# Better With Age

## Your Blueprint for Staying Smart, Strong, and Happy for Life

Robin Porter

**Spry**Publishing

This edition is published by
Spry Publishing LLC
315 East Eisenhower Pkwy, Ste 2
Ann Arbor, MI 48108 USA

Printed and bound in the United States of America.

10   9   8   7   6   5   4   3   2   1

Library of Congress Control Number: 2014936023

Paperback ISBN: 978-1-938170-49-2
eBook ISBN: 978-1-938170-50-8

# Contents

# Introduction

## The Search Continues

For centuries, humans have been seeking it. We've sailed across oceans, trekked long distances to remote villages, and scaled mountains to find it. We've consulted shamans, priests, and yogis trying to uncover its secrets. We've tried herbs, potions, and "miracle" foods in hopes of obtaining it. What is this elusive thing we seem so desperate to find? Some might call it the fountain of youth or a "cure" for old age, but what we're really searching for is a way to stay young and prolong our lives.

The interest in extending longevity is as old as humankind itself. The subject was explored in Greek mythology and pondered by ancient philosophers. For nearly 5,000 years, traditional Chinese medicine has prescribed meditation, yoga, and herbal remedies to promote health and lengthen life—practices that continue to be used today. In 1550, one of the first known books on longevity, entitled *The Art of Living Long*, was written by Luigi Cornaro, who suggested that life could be extended through moderation. Many would agree this is still good advice. Since then, scientists, demographers, gerontologists, and other experts have been working tirelessly to uncover the secrets to a longer life.

Today we have an entire industry devoted to antiaging—one that is growing rapidly. Research from Global Industry Analysts projects that the U.S. market for antiaging products and treatments will expand from $80 billion in 2013 to more than $114 billion by the year 2015, fueled by our desire to slow, stop, or even reverse the effects of aging. From wrinkle creams and cosmetic surgery, to dietary supplements and hormone therapy, there are many who are eager to capitalize on our obsession with youth. In fact, there have been so many products and treatments promising antiaging miracles over the years, it prompted the National Institute on Aging (NIA) to issue a warning to consumers to be skeptical of exaggerated claims. According to the NIA, the best advice for living longer goes like this: eat a healthy diet, exercise regularly, and don't smoke.

Despite our modern medical marvels and the emergence of a variety of antiaging specialists, including biogerontologists whose goal is to "extend a healthy life span," it seems there is still no miracle cure for aging. Indeed, there is widespread disagreement within the medical establishment as to whether such a "cure" exists. But the search continues.

## Taking Control

In the meantime, we can take matters into our own hands. Aging may be inevitable, but how we age is largely up to us. In fact, there is a great deal we can do to improve this phase of our life. While scientists work to discover the role that genes play in aging, we know that only about 20 to 30 percent of how long we live, as well as our health during those years, is dictated by genetics. The other 70 to 80 percent is determined by lifestyle and environmental factors, including diet, exercise, education, healthcare, interaction with others, and even attitude.

For instance, the number one killer of both men and women in the United States is heart disease, the majority of which is preventable. Chronic illnesses such as type 2 diabetes and high blood pressure, which shorten lives and decrease the quality of life in older adults, are also largely avoidable and can be controlled with proper treatment. Though the scientific community may disagree on how to prevent the effects of aging, most would agree that we can significantly influence how well we age.

In addition to health considerations, planning for your senior years can also improve the quality of those years. Saving for retirement, downsizing, choosing the best place to live, maintaining social connections, putting your estate in order, and making end-of-life decisions are important factors in the aging process. In other words, *aging well doesn't just happen—it requires planning and thoughtful decision making.* Yet, all too often, these decisions are made after a health crisis or accident occurs, when we are least able to make well-researched, careful choices.

The goal of this book is to help you prepare for your senior years, considering some of the plans and actions you should be taking in your 50s, 60s, 70s, 80s, and beyond. The information contained within these pages is not meant to reveal the mysteries of human longevity, but rather empower you to live an active, engaged life; to make your senior years the healthiest, happiest possible. To that end, we've gathered expert advice from many fields, including financial planning, elder law, healthcare, nutrition, and physical therapy. You'll also find stories from people in different stages of life to help educate and inspire. And, of course, who better to guide our journey than those who are living a long life while maintaining their vitality—so look for "Words of Wisdom" sprinkled throughout.

## Lessons Learned

Speaking of folks who have lived a long life, in 2008, the National Geographic Society published a book entitled *The Blue Zones* that profiled four distinct areas of the world with high concentrations of some of the longest-lived people. These people are unique not only because they reached the age of 100 or more, but they also exhibited "amazing vigor," remaining healthy and active into their advanced years. What's their secret?

This study of the world's healthiest long-lived people teaches us there is not one secret, but rather many factors that contribute to aging well. While one woman credits her health and longevity to a strict vegetarian diet and yoga, a man attributes his vitality to hard work and a daily Scotch; still another person believes strong faith and family ties are key. There are, of course, some common denominators among these remarkable people, who have not only managed to live long lives, but fulfilling, purposeful lives.

In the end, our life span is determined by a combination of factors, including genetics, environment, and lifestyle choices. But is longevity really the most important issue? As Steven N. Austad, Ph.D., author of *Why We Age: What Science Is Discovering About the Human Body's Journey Through Life* states: "The question is—and here's where I think the best health practices are really important—if you live to be 100 years old, what sort of 100-year-old are you going to be?" Aging and many of its effects are unavoidable, but how we plan for and handle these changes are up to each of us.

## Nine Lessons from the Blue Zones

Although the Blue Zones are distinctly different areas scattered around the world—Sardinia, Italy; Okinawa, Japan; Loma Linda, California; and Nicoya, Costa Rica—they have something in common: they are home to the world's longest-lived people. More importantly, these people live healthy, active lives well into their 90s and 100s. They manage to live longer and better, not through medical intervention or miracle cures, but with these simple everyday habits:

- **Regular physical activity**—They don't run marathons or do power lifting, but they do engage in daily low-intensity physical activity, such as walking and gardening, which is often part of their work or lifestyle.
- **Calorie reduction**—Though the menu is different in each Blue Zone, they all consume fewer daily calories than many other parts of the word. They don't "go on diets," but naturally eat less—and what they do eat is leaner. Okinawans stop eating when their stomachs are 80 percent full, which is a way of eating mindfully.
- **Less meat and processed food**—Most centenarians in these Blue Zones never had the chance to develop a taste for processed food because it was not available. Meat was also a luxury, which was eaten only occasionally. As a result, their diets consist primarily of beans and tofu, whole grains, nuts, fruits, and vegetables.
- **Red wine in moderation**—Studies show that drinking a glass of beer, wine, or spirits each day can provide health benefits. Red wine in particular contains polyphenols that may help fight arteriosclerosis (clogged arteries) and boost antioxidants.
- **Purposeful living**—The people in each Blue Zone have a strong sense of purpose or reason for getting up every morning. In another study, individuals who had a clear goal in life lived longer and stayed

mentally sharper than those who did not. Your purpose could be a job or hobby, children or grandchildren, or learning something new, which has the added bonus of exercising your brain.

- **Stress relief**—Each of these cultures has a regular way of reducing stress, from taking a break every afternoon to rest and socialize with friends, to family nature walks and meditation. Reducing stress lessens chronic inflammation that damages the body.

- **Spiritual connections**—Studies indicate that those who attend religious services or practice their faith have a longer life expectancy. It doesn't matter what faith or spiritual practice you engage in, as long as you connect regularly. Spiritual connections lower rates of cardiovascular disease, depression, stress, and suicide and boost the immune system. In addition, those who attend church are more likely to adopt other healthful behaviors.

- **Family first**—Blue Zone centenarians build their lives around family—familial duty, ritual, and togetherness. Even work is seen as something you do for your family. In return, their children and grandchildren love and care for them as they grow old. With the help of their families, these elders eat healthier, have lower levels of stress, and suffer fewer accidents. They also exhibit sharper mental and social skills.

- **Shared communities**—It makes sense that people who practice healthy habits are more likely to stick to those habits when they are surrounded by others who do the same. In addition, social connect-edness is strongly linked to longevity. A positive social network can relieve stress and boost happiness, as well as provide both mental and physical support.

*Source:* Dan Buettner, *The Blue Zones* (National Geographic Society, 2008).

# CHAPTER ONE

# Choosing to Age Well

*"Aging seems to be the only available way
to live a long life."*
—KITTY O'NEILL COLLINS

## The Miracle of You

*On a balmy spring evening, Agnes sat listening to the haunting sounds of bagpipes and watching the sun sink slowly over the lake, ribbons of orange and purple rippling on the water's surface. Her family had hired the bagpipe player, donned in a traditional kilt, as a surprise addition to Agnes's 90th birthday party—a nod to their Scottish heritage. When the music ended and the sky had faded to a soft pink glow, Agnes stood, leaning heavily on her cane, and gave each of her three children, seven grandchildren, and nine great grandchildren a hearty hug. She felt like the luckiest woman in the world.*

*"When people ask me how old I am, I tell them the truth—I'm 90 and proud of it!" declared Agnes with a wide grin. "I have no idea why people lie about their age. Every year on this earth is something to celebrate."*

*Sobering a bit, she added, "Of course, life isn't all sunshine and roses. Looking back, there was pain and sadness, and loneliness at times. I lost my husband too soon, and my brother died of a heart condition when he was just a young man. These days they probably would have been able to save him. We suffered through some hard times during the Depression, and lost dear friends and neighbors in the war. I suppose everyone experiences hardships, some more than others, but in the end, it's the love and beauty I remember most."*

*Agnes, who still feels a jolt of joy when the first spring flower peeks through the snow and the hummingbirds return to her feeder, believes the secret to lifelong happiness is the ability to appreciate the simple pleasures and be grateful. Using her fingers, which are bent with arthritis, she ticked off a few of the many things for which she is thankful, including sunsets, good books, summer tomatoes, chocolate, and a lovable mutt named Chaucer—and, of course, her large, adoring family.*

*As the evening wore on, one of Agnes's great granddaughters who had recently graduated from college sat down beside her and asked for some counsel. Patting her knee fondly, Agnes replied, "Well, first be thankful for the opportunities you've been given. I always wished I had continued my education. Never stop learning and growing, and being interested in the world around you. Find someone special to love and cherish every moment together. And, don't waste your time looking for miracles, because life is a miracle—live it accordingly."*

Agnes is right. The fact that you are alive today is nothing short of a miracle. Some scientists calculate the probability of your existence today at approximately one in 400 trillion. Taking it a step farther, doctor and author Ali Binazir performed a series of calculations that estimate your chances of being here at nearly zero. First he looked at the likelihood of your parents meeting and having a child, which are about one in 40 million. Next, he projected the odds of one particular egg being fertilized (out of an average of 100,000 for each woman) by one particular sperm (out of the nearly 12 trillion produced by each man during his lifetime), each genetically unique, at one in 400 quadrillion. But that's only a small part of your personal story.

Consider the long chain of unlikely events that had to occur throughout the ages: You are a result of many generations of people who survived such challenges as war, famine, and disease and reproduced successfully. When you factor in your ancestry, Binazir contends that the odds of you existing (as you) is more like one in $10^{2,685,000}$ (that's 10 with 2,685,000 zeros after it!). But with a number that large, why quibble over a few zeros? Let's just say that beating such staggering odds should give us pause to contemplate how lucky we are to be here. So, as Agnes wisely advised, we should live life accordingly.

## An Appetite for Life

The choices we make throughout our lives have a profound effect on our health, happiness, and quality of life. When we're young the choices seem limitless, spread out before us like an all-you-can-eat buffet. With great hunger, we make decisions regarding education, career, marriage, and family and often sample many different interests and ideas until we find those that satisfy us. However, as we age, there is often a tendency to feel that our options are limited. For instance, we might reach a certain age and think we're "too old" to continue our education,

switch careers, or pursue a dream; or perhaps we believe it's "too late" to change our lifestyle or improve our health. Yet nothing could be farther from the truth.

Research shows that those who maintain their vitality well into their advanced years are those who continue to have an appetite for life. They understand that we are never too old to stop moving forward, making improvements, and living with purpose—and never too young to start! Getting older brings changes, but you can prepare for those changes and make the most of your senior years, no matter what phase of life you're in. We can start by looking at how aging has changed, what it means to age well, and why it requires some planning.

Like Agnes, Nola (Hill) Ochs always loved learning and wanted to attend college, but young women were not encouraged to continue their education in her day. Instead, she got married, raised a family, and worked on the farm, but she never lost her yearning for knowledge. So, in 1972, at the age of 60, she started taking correspondence courses in hopes of obtaining her bachelor's degree. Thirty-five years later, at the age of 95, Ochs graduated alongside her granddaughter, earning a general studies degree with an emphasis in history. In 2010, at the age of 98, she received her master's degree. Of her accomplishment, she said simply, "It was something I wanted to do. It gave me a feeling of satisfaction." After graduation, Ochs planned on applying for a job as a graduate teaching assistant.

### Truth *and* Consequences

Aging is a natural and unavoidable part of life. We begin the process at birth and continue to age with each passing day. Thankfully, both the quantity and quality of those days are likely to be greater than ever before, as people are living longer and generally healthier lives. According to the U.S. Centers for Disease Control and Prevention (CDC), the average life expectancy (from birth) for someone living in the United States is currently 78.7 years. If you reach the age of 65, you have a good chance of extending your life span to 83 years. Of course, these are only averages. Nowadays, we are seeing more and more people live well into their 90s and even celebrate a century or more of living. Indeed, though still a small percentage, centenarians are the fastest growing segment of the U.S. population.

Over the past century, life expectancy has increased by nearly 30 years. A man born in 1900 could expect to live, on average, to the age of 48, while a woman might reach 51. This seems young by today's standards, but it's a vast improvement over earlier civilizations, such as the Roman Empire, which had an approximate life expectancy of just 22 to 25 years old! Nowhere are the advantages of modern-day living more apparent than in our improved longevity.

The lives of our ancestors were shortened by a long list of factors, including poor hygiene, unclean water, inadequate nutrition, and lack of medical care, which often led to infectious diseases. In fact, infectious diseases such as influenza, pneumonia, tuberculosis, and gastrointestinal infections were the leading causes of death in 1900. Today, only two of those illnesses, influenza and pneumonia, even make the list of leading causes of death in the United States, tying for ninth place. Instead, chronic conditions such as heart disease, cancer, noninfectious respiratory problems (e.g., fibrosis), and stroke have taken the top spots. Thanks to improvements in public health, nutrition, and medicine, particularly antibiotics and vaccines, we have reduced childhood mortality rates and wiped out many of the maladies faced by earlier generations—and we continue to learn.

Consider, for example, that in the not-so-distant past, the medical community believed life-shortening ailments such as heart disease, hypertension, and strokes were unavoidable side effects of the aging process. We now know these problems are, to a large extent, preventable and, if they do occur, can often be treated successfully. As Agnes pointed out, her brother's heart condition may not have been fatal if he had been born a few decades later. And, it's not just longevity that has improved: Better education, enhanced nutrition, and advanced medical treatments are helping people age with fewer disabilities and chronic health issues overall. Modern medicine offers a long list of life-enhancing and life-extending procedures—from

## The Vulnerable Years

Though longevity rates have improved dramatically during the twentieth century, American longevity has actually dropped since 1979, compared to some other nations, according to the National Academy of Sciences. On average, Australian, Japanese, Italian, and French men and women are outliving Americans by four to six years. Researchers also noted that Americans seem to be at their most vulnerable between the ages of 55 and 75. These are the years when the cumulative effects of poor eating habits, lack of exercise, and skipped health screenings take their toll, resulting in a large number of deaths due to heart disease, diabetes, lung disease, and cancer that has gone undetected. However, if Americans reach the age of 75 and beyond, they have a good chance of living well into their 90s and even 100s. The trend emphasizes the importance of healthy lifestyle choices at every life stage.

replacing worn-out knees and broken hips to implanting pace-makers and transplanting organs. All of which is good news.

Greater longevity does, however, have some consequences. According to "The State of Aging and Health in America," a 2013 special report from the CDC, the population of older Americans may be expanding faster than our healthcare system can handle. Approximately 80 million baby boomers—who began turning 65 in 2011 and can expect to live longer lives—are creating a massive shift in demographics. By 2030, it's estimated that 1 in 5 Americans will be a senior citizen, nearly double the 12 percent we had in 2000.

Despite our medical advancements, the human body will still wear out over time. So, the longer you live, the more susceptible you become to disabilities and frailties, which necessitate more specialized and long-term care. At current growth rates, the demand for these services will outpace supply. There is already a shortage of physicians and nurses who specialize in elder care and the need continues to increase. The American Geriatric Society tells us there are currently only 7,500 geriatric specialists in the United States, and growth in this area of expertise is sluggish. Meanwhile, the need for geriatricians will expand to approximately 30,000 by 2030. It's clear that, as a society, we will be challenged to find innovative ways to treat and support an aging population—and to pay for this care.

Financial resources play an important part in the longevity issue. Living longer after retirement means you need to stash away more savings, not only to maintain an acceptable standard of living, but to provide for additional care and services as you age. Unfortunately, reports indicate that baby boomers are not preparing for their retirement years as well as they should be.

When Jeanne Louise Calment (1875–1997) celebrated her 110th birthday, she became the oldest known living human (as verified by modern documentation). But, it wasn't her age that people found the most amazing; it was her upbeat attitude toward aging and life that captivated audiences around the world. Active and clear-minded, she quipped to the press, "I had to wait 110 years to become famous. I want to enjoy it as long as possible." She went on to reach the amazing age of 122!

This lack of planning contradicts survey results in which those 65 and older rank "maintaining independence" as their top priority.

Still, when asked, most people say they would like to live a long life, with this caveat: as long as they can age well.

### What Is Aging Well?

Vibrant centenarians such as Ms. Calment are certainly examples of aging well, which is sometimes referred to as "successful aging." But, aging well can mean many things. What constitutes successful aging differs from one culture to another and even from individual to individual. In general, Americans define aging well as:

- **Remaining independent** for as long as possible.
- **Being healthy and mobile** enough to enjoy hobbies and time with family.
- **Feeling useful,** whether through continued work, volunteer activities, or family obligations.
- **Having enough money** to live comfortably after retirement.

However, as mentioned, there seems to be a wide gap between what people say is important and what actually happens.

Simply put, most Americans are not planning effectively to achieve these goals. Consider the following:

- According to the National Bureau of Economic Research, only 40 percent of Americans have tried to figure out how much to save for retirement. Only 51 percent say they have a retirement account through an employer and only 28 percent had a separate retirement account.
- The majority of people say they want control over their health decisions, but only 25 to 30 percent of those surveyed have an advanced health directive or living will.
- Less than one-third of adults have discussed their end-of-life wishes with children or other family members.
- Though the key to preventing chronic illnesses such as heart disease is managing risk factors—high blood pressure, high cholesterol, and high blood glucose levels—many adults in the United States do not get regular health screenings, which can detect these problems at the earliest stages, allowing for lifestyle changes and/or proper treatment.

Considering that the resources and benefits available for seniors today may or may not be available in the future, this lack of planning becomes even more troubling.

## A Change in Attitude

Perhaps one of the reasons we don't do a good job of planning for our senior years is because growing old is something about which we don't like to think, so we continually put it off. For instance, the majority of people surveyed by the American Association of Retired Persons (AARP) believed that an advanced health directive and durable power of attorney were only necessary for "very sick or very old people."

"That's a common misperception," says Christopher J. Berry, Certified Elder Law Attorney. "In reality, these documents should be prepared while we are healthy and our decisions are not complicated by age, illness, medications, or end-of-life emotions. Making these plans provides peace of mind for yourself and your loved ones. In fact, medical powers of attorney and financial powers of attorney should be prepared when you turn 18 and are legally an adult. You never know when life will throw you a curve ball."

Of course, as Berry points out, these documents are not just for older folks; accidents and unexpected health crises can happen at any age. We have all heard the heartbreaking stories of people who suddenly lose a loved one and find themselves trying to untangle a financial and legal mess. While most people understand that proper planning can prevent these problems, many still fail to make those plans.

Our reluctance may also have something to do with the youth-centered culture in which we live. Youth is celebrated, while growing old is often portrayed negatively, as something to be dreaded and avoided. Just look at the billions of dollars generated by the sale of antiaging products—from wrinkle creams and cosmetic surgery meant to maintain our youthful appearance, to vitamins and herbal remedies that promise to

The ancient Greek philosopher Epicurus thought that "old age was the pinnacle of life," while recognizing that each stage in life has its own qualities and advantages, as well as disadvantages. Successful aging comes when we are able to make the most of both the virtues and the vices.

slow down or even reverse the aging process. In fact, the market for antiaging products and treatments is one of the fastest growing business segments in our nation.

In many cultures, including those with a high concentration of centenarians, aging comes with a badge of honor. Seniors are respected for their wisdom and given a sense of purpose by being asked to help raise children and contribute to the family household. Indeed, one of the secrets of successful aging is adopting a positive attitude about growing old. As we plan for late life, we should not think of aging as something to fear and revile—an inevitable decline—but rather a time of new beginnings, as well as intellectual and spiritual growth. Our senior years can be a time of productivity and fulfillment—with a little preparation.

### Never Too Late

Chronological age is just a number—not your identity. Look around and you'll discover many inspiring examples of people pursuing dreams and achieving success late in life, refusing to be defined by their age. Some notable illustrations:

- At 77 years old, Senator John Glenn was the oldest person to board a U.S. space shuttle. When asked if he thought he was too old for the mission, he responded, "Too many people, when they get old, think that they have to live by the calendar."
- Anna Mary Robertson Moses, better known as Grandma Moses, didn't pick up a paintbrush until she was in her 70s, after arthritis forced her to give up a career in embroidery. By the time she died in 1961 at the age of 101, she had become one of America's most beloved artists, her paintings adorning the walls of museums around the world. Grandma Moses had no formal art training, but she painted every day, completing more than a thousand works of art in 25

years. As Moses said (and demonstrated), "One is never too old to succeed in life."

- The best-selling author Laura Ingalls Wilder didn't publish her first book until she was 64. She spent most of her life as a teacher and a farmer's wife, occasionally writing articles on farming and rural life in the early 1900s. With her daughter's encouragement, she started writing about her pioneering childhood and published *Little House in the Big Woods* in 1932 (which later inspired the popular television series *Little House on the Prairie*).

- Despite health issues, including diabetes and arthritis, Ray Kroc set out to make McDonald's a household name at the age of 52. But first he spent 17 years as a paper cup salesman and another 17 years selling a machine called the Multimixer, which could whip up five milkshakes at once. Though the invention was designed for drug stores with soda fountains, Kroc had more success selling the device to hamburger joints and drive-ins, which is how he met Maurice and Richard McDonald. The McDonald brothers owned a few restaurants in California and Arizona, but Kroc suggested they franchise their operation on a national scale and volunteered to take on the task. Seven years later, he became the owner of a franchise that would sell more than a billion hamburgers by 1963. Today, McDonald's is the most successful fast food operation in the world.

- As a young housewife, Julia Child was not a particularly good cook—she noted that she didn't even know what a shallot was. When she moved to France with her husband, she began looking for something to occupy herself and decided to learn how to make French cuisine. She studied at the Cordon Bleu cooking school and fell in love. She once wrote, "To think it has taken me 40 years to find my true passion." It took another decade and numerous rejections before she published her famous book *Mastering the Art of French Cooking* and began her long-running PBS program *The French Chef* at the age of 51.

- In 1994, when he was nearly 76, Nelson Mandela was elected president of South Africa in the first election open to all races in that country's history. After a life-long struggle against racial segregation and nearly 27 years in prison, Mandela became instrumental in abolishing apartheid in his homeland. He was an activist, politician, lawyer, and philanthropist who received the Nobel Peace Prize in 1993 and worked to end poverty through the Nelson Mandela Foundation until his death at the age of 95.

- After teaching at St. Mary's School for Girls in India for 17 years, Mother Teresa experienced what she referred to as "the call within the call" to work with the poor in the streets of Calcutta. At age 38, she left the Sisters of Loretto to move into the slums, where she started a school and tended to the sick and dying. At the age of 40, she established the Missionaries of Charity, which eventually became a worldwide organization consisting of more than 4,500 sisters running hospices, homes for the sick, soup kitchens, orphanages, and schools. Mother Teresa received the Nobel Peace Prize at the age of 69 and worked tirelessly until her death at age 87.

- Popular actor, film director, and producer Clint Eastwood is still working hard at the age of 83. He began his career in 1959, but didn't receive an Academy Award until he was 62 years old. At 73, he launched his critically acclaimed directing career, which earned him another Oscar. Eastwood sums up his philosophy about aging in this quote: "As we grow older, we must discipline ourselves to continue expanding, broadening, learning, keeping our minds active and open."

Benjamin Franklin helped draft the Declaration of Independence and signed it at the age of 70, which incidentally was the same age as Ronald Reagan when he was sworn in as the 40th president of the United States—just two more examples of late-in-life achievements. But you don't have to be famous to be successful; every day, ordinary folks are finding passion and purpose in the second half of their lives and redefining what it means to age well.

## The Importance of Planning

Like most things in life, aging well does not happen by accident—it requires some planning. The following chapters cover key aspects of preparing for each decade of your senior years, including money matters, legal issues, health factors, and tips for staying vibrant. We cannot control every element of the aging process, but we can positively influence many facets. By avoiding unhealthy habits and taking better care of ourselves, we can stave off many ailments that lead to disabilities, reduce the quality of our senior years, and shorten lives. By saving for retirement, we can make our senior years more fulfilling and enjoyable. And, by putting our affairs in order, we can reduce some of the stress associated with growing older, make more informed decisions, and ensure that our wishes are carried out. In other words, we can choose to age well.

Poet Maya Angelou wrote, "Living life is like constructing a building: if you start wrong, you'll end wrong." As we embark on our senior years, it's a good idea to start with a plan or blueprint of sorts. Along the way we're sure to make alterations, add details here and there, and perhaps undertake some major renovations—all the while steadily building the second half of our lives. We don't know what the finished project will look like, but let's begin by laying a strong foundation.

## Words of Wisdom . . .

*For three generations, Lydia's family has lived in the same community, and with nearly a century of life behind her, Lydia has seen some tremendous transformations.*

*"I was recently asked to speak about life here in the 1920s at the library, and I've also participated in discussion panels at the university," said Lydia proudly. "I guess when you're as old as I am you become a walking history book! This used to be a small town, where you knew all the shopkeepers by name and all the kids went to the same school. Times have certainly changed, but I'm just so grateful to have lived to see so many truly amazing things in the world."*

*As schoolchildren, Lydia and her classmates were invited to help fill up seats at the new university stadium and cheer on the football team—a venue that now routinely holds well over 100,000 fans. She also recalled graduating during the Great Depression, when the school had no money for caps and gowns, and learning the importance of service from her parents who were both active in the community; her father organized the first African-American Boy Scouts troop in town and her mother worked with young girls at the local community center. Lydia married when she was 19 and had four children— she also became a member of the "sandwich generation" long before that term was coined.*

*"I had taken a course in home nursing, so when my mother had a stroke, and then my father became ill, I took charge of their care," she recounted. "My children were young at the time, so for many years, my only activities were taking care of family, which is really the most important thing in life."*

*After Lydia's parents passed away, she took a job planning and preparing meals for a local doctor and his family, and eventually worked in his office, as well. Her favorite job, however, was managing the dining room of a well-known social club, where she worked for 20 years. But retirement didn't slow Lydia down.*

In addition to panel discussions, she is on the church committee to plan monthly senior activities, and she participates in all the trips and events. "I've always been active," Lydia said. "As a girl, I was on the track team, and played baseball and field hockey. We had no cars, so we walked everywhere. Now, I use a walker and don't get around as well as I used to, but I don't let that get me down. Even if you're slow, it doesn't mean you should stop moving!"

When it comes to her longevity, Lydia is a firm believer in eating well and staying active. As for her remarkable vibrancy at 97, she offers this advice, "Have a positive attitude, and surround yourself with good friends and family. Don't lose interest in things or close yourself off. I like to stay current on social issues and politics. I like to read, and I'm still a big football fan!"

# CHAPTER TWO

# Laying the Foundation: Your 50s

*"Grow old along with me! The best is yet to be."*
—ROBERT BROWNING

## I'm Too Young for That

*When Jan found a copy of* AARP The Magazine *in her mailbox, she thought there was some mistake. Maybe it was intended for her mother? Or, perhaps this was her husband's idea of a birthday joke, since she had just celebrated her 50th. But no, the publication geared toward seniors was addressed to her. How can I be old enough to be a "senior?" thought Jan, when she was still working full-time and attending her son's high school football games. Like Jan, many people don't consider themselves to be senior citizens in their 50s—and they certainly don't feel old.*

*In 2014, the last of the baby boomers will reach age 50, officially putting this large segment of Americans, born between 1946 and 1964, in their senior years. Life expectancy has increased by an average of 12 years since the first boomers were born, along with "health expectancy" or number of years we can expect to live without health problems or disabilities—which begs the question: What will we do with this extra decade or more of life?*

Some might say 50 is the new 40. A majority of those in their 50s are still engrossed in careers, with no immediate plans for retiring. And because people are waiting longer to start families, a large number still have school-aged children at home during this decade. Another sizeable segment of this group known as the sandwich generation is raising children *and* caring for elderly parents. All of which means that instead of slowing down, many 50-somethings are busier than ever. Thankfully, a good portion of those in their 50s are healthy and active enough to keep up with these demands.

However, at 50, issues that once seemed distant are now visible on the horizon. If you haven't already made plans for retirement or spent time thinking about end-of-life issues, there is no time like the present—whether you are in a position to have important conversations with elderly parents regarding their affairs or contemplating your own wishes. In fact, the decisions and plans we make in our 50s will set the stage for our senior years.

> Novelist and dramatist Victor Hugo once said, "Forty is the old age of youth; fifty is the youth of old age." As we embark on our senior years, we should take advantage of this "youthfulness" to plan for late life.

## Money Matters

Despite our best intentions, many Americans don't get serious about saving for retirement until midlife or later. At that point, some people may begin to panic when they read the amount experts say they "should" have saved by this age. It's easy to get discouraged and even adopt a "why bother" attitude. However, it's not too late, and doing something is always better than doing nothing. If you've been saving and investing for retirement, now is the time to make assessments and possibly step up your efforts. If you haven't begun the process, start by taking small, manageable steps. Financial experts recommend laying out a road map for retirement that includes the following:

- **Run projections** using a retirement calculator (available online), which can give you a broad overview. Don't forget to estimate future healthcare costs, particularly if you are planning to retire before Medicare age.
- **Sit down with a financial planner** (if you haven't done so already) and create a financial inventory. Then project when you want to retire, keeping in mind there is nothing magic about ages 62 or 65, and see if you are on target to meet your financial needs. The average family requires 70 to 90 percent of preretirement income, but this amount varies with individual situations.
- **Refinance your mortgage** to pay it off sooner, if possible.
- **Get a handle on spending.** The best way to save is to spend less. Create a retirement budget worksheet that includes regular contributions to your retirement savings.
- **Maximize your retirement contributions.** In recent years, the allowable contribution amounts for both 401(k) accounts and individual retirement accounts (IRAs) were raised. In 2014, an employee age 50 and older can now contribute up to $23,000 annually into a 401(k) account, and an additional $6,500 into an IRA.
- **Educate yourself.** Understand your investment options, attend seminars, and read books on the subject. Take advantage of free retirement planning seminars offered by financial advisors and community centers.
- **Focus on your career.** Your earning power is one of

your biggest assets, so don't be too quick to give it up. It may mean switching careers.

- **Evaluate your investments.** Shift your investment focus to strategies that help maximize lifetime income and reduce risk.
- **Evaluate your insurance needs,** including life, disability, and long-term care insurance. The best time to purchase this type of insurance is when you are healthy.

"It's also important to note that at age 50, employees who participate in certain qualified retirement plans are able to begin making annual 'catch-up' contributions in addition to their normal contributions," says Michael Johnson, Certified Financial Planner® (CFP®), CPWA®. "Those who participate in 401(k), 403(b), and 457 plans can add an additional $5,500 per year, while those in simple IRA or simple 401(k) plans can make a catch-up contribution of up to $2,500. And, finally, those who participate in traditional IRAs can set aside an additional $1,000 a year. It's a good way to jump start your retirement savings."

When it comes to financial planning, another milestone to consider is age 59½; that's when you are able to start making withdrawals from *some* qualified retirement plans without incurring a 10 percent tax penalty. To find out if this applies to your particular plan, as well as whether it makes good economic sense to begin making these withdrawals, you should consult with your financial planner.

*It seemed like only yesterday when Kate was sitting in front of her adolescent daughter, who was squirming uncomfortably in her seat, having "the talk." Now, here she was years later, having an equally difficult conversation with her adult daughter, who was once again squirming in her seat. This time, the topic was end-of-life wishes.*

*Despite her daughter's discomfort, Kate forged ahead because she understood the importance of broaching this sensitive subject. Kate, who was also caring for her elderly father, knew from experience that the time to have this discussion was when she was healthy. After her dad had suddenly suffered a debilitating stroke, Kate and her sister were left with some very difficult decisions and no direction.*

*"My dad didn't believe in talking about things," lamented Kate. "He had no plans or instructions, which made the situation very hard for us. I vowed that I wouldn't put my own kids through that kind of stress."*

*Kate understood that being proactive is the best way to reduce stress and avoid future problems for all parties. Next on her agenda was a meeting with their financial planner to assess their retirement savings.*

## Legal Issues

As Kate's story illustrates, now is the time to put advance directives in place, including a living will and a durable power of attorney (also known as a healthcare proxy or patient advocate designation). Too often, we wait until there is a health crisis before creating these important documents. In fact, it's estimated that nearly 44 percent of those 45 to 64 years old do not have a will, even though we acknowledge the importance of having one. In 2013, The Conversation Project, a national campaign aimed at helping people initiate discussions about end-of-life wishes, conducted a survey that revealed that 94 percent of Americans felt these conversations were important, but less than one-third actually had such dialogues with loved ones. When asked why they hadn't broached the subject, respondents listed a variety of reasons, including: "I'm not sick yet," "I might upset my loved ones," "It never seems like the right time," and "I don't know how to start the conversation."

While death and dying are still taboo subjects to many, they become increasingly important as we reach midlife—not only to us, but to our children and, in some cases, our aging parents. Experts agree that the best time to discuss end-of-life care and wishes is *before* a life-threatening illness or health crisis, when you are not under duress. By preparing in advance, you can reduce stress for yourself and your loved ones and make educated decisions that may include input from those closest to you. And, because unexpected end-of-life situations can happen at any age, *all* adults should have advance directives in place.

In the simplest terms, advance directives describe your preferences regarding treatment if you're faced with a serious accident or illness. These legal documents speak for you if you are unable to speak for yourself. Your family and physicians will consult your advance directives if you are unable to make your own healthcare decisions, thereby reducing confusion and disagreement. Advance directives typically include:

- **A living will**—This written document specifically outlines the types of medical treatments and life-sustaining measures you want and don't want, such as artificial breathing (respiration and ventilation), feeding tubes, or resuscitation. In some states, living wills may be called healthcare declarations or healthcare directives. It's also important to note that laws differ by state. For instance, some states do not have living will statutes, in which a clear and convincing declaration of end-of-life wishes must be documented, typically in the medical power of attorney, while others do.

- **Medical or healthcare power of attorney (POA)**—This legal document, which may also be called a Durable Power of Attorney, designates an individual (referred to as your healthcare agent or proxy) to make medical decisions for you if you are unable to do so. (Note: This is different from a power of attorney authorizing someone to make financial transactions for you.)

- **Do not resuscitate (DNR) order**—This is a written request to forgo cardiopulmonary resuscitation (CPR) if your heart stops or you stop breathing. Advance directives do not have to include a DNR, and you aren't required to have advance directives in place to request a DNR. Your physician can put a DNR order in your medical chart. It's important to note that many states require a separate DNR form, which is state-specific and bears the signature of a physician (see chapter 5 for more details).

These legalities may seem overwhelming or even a bit depressing to consider, but they are necessary to ensure that your end-of-life wishes are carried out and help your loved ones during an already difficult time. While most of these documents are readily available online, consulting an attorney or, more specifically, an attorney who specializes in elder law is highly recommended, as laws and terminology differ by state. These professionals can walk you through the process, explain your options, and answer questions along the way. They can also help you plan for all the "what ifs" that you may not have considered before. The cost of preparing these documents is generally very affordable. However, if fees are a concern, many communities offer free or low-cost legal resources to help you draft these important documents. The National Elder Law Foundation (nelf.org) can help you find a local attorney. If possible, select a *certified* elder law attorney, which is considered the gold standard in the industry.

Keep in mind, documents don't replace conversations! Simply stashing these documents away in a safe deposit box somewhere doesn't help anyone. It's vital to have open, honest conversations with your spouse, adult children, or other family members who may be involved in future caregiving or decision making. Share these documents with them (all parties should have a copy) and explain your wishes in person, if possible. Before appointing a POA, be sure that individual understands your requests and is willing to accept the responsibility. It's also a good idea to review these documents every year or so, as things change.

If you are finding it difficult to initiate these conversations with aging parents or adult children, as the case may be, the Conversation Project offers some tips for getting started at www.theconversationproject.org. Groups such as the AARP and the Area Agencies on Aging are also good resources for how to get started and what topics to consider. Many people note that once the end-of-life subject is broached, this conversation can be one of the most meaningful talks they've ever had with their loved ones.

## Health Factors
### *Prevention Is the Best Medicine*
As discussed, many of the illnesses that were once associated with aging are largely avoidable and can be successfully treated. The keys are prevention and early diagnosis. Quite simply, the choices we make in our 50s regarding our health can greatly affect the quality of life in our late years. Even if you've neglected your health up to this point, it's never too late to make improvements. Now is the time to take control.

### *Smoking*
Let's start with the culprit behind most preventable causes of death and disease in the United States—smoking. You may be familiar with the warnings regarding emphysema, bronchitis, and lung cancer, but did you know that smoking is also linked to heart disease and stroke? In fact, more smokers die from heart attacks than respiratory problems, and among those under 50, cigarette smoking is the number one risk factor for cardio-

vascular disease. Smoking damages the walls of your arteries, making them more susceptible to atherosclerosis (narrowing and hardening of the arteries), decreases circulation, increases blood pressure, reduces oxygen levels in the blood, and ups your chances of developing blood clots. Evidence also suggests that smoking contributes to unhealthy cholesterol levels.

And it's not just cigarettes that are cause for concern—chewing tobacco and other products containing nicotine, such as smokeless cigarettes, can also be detrimental to your health. If you're a tobacco user, the best thing you can do to improve your health is to stop, now! Even if you've smoked for many years, the health benefits of kicking the habit are immediate and improve over time. Within 20 minutes of your last cigarette, nicotine stops constricting blood vessels, your heart rate slows down, and your blood pressure decreases. After 8 to 10 hours without lighting up, your circulation begins to improve, carbon monoxide levels in your blood drop, and oxygen levels increase (your organs will thank you). After 24 smoke-free hours, your heart attack risk is reduced, and the body continues to heal with each passing day. Studies show that after a year of quitting, cardiovascular risks related to smoking are cut in half.

Of course, giving up tobacco is not easy. Nicotine is as addictive as heroin, and it often takes repeated attempts for folks to kick the habit for good. The good news is there are many tools available to help you succeed, such as nicotine replacement gum, lozenges, and patches. Though many of these aids are available over-the-counter, the best place to begin is with your healthcare provider, who can guide you in the process and possibly prescribe medications that reduce cravings and withdrawal symptoms. It's important to follow directions carefully when using these products to avoid potential complications such as nicotine poisoning and interactions with other medications. To get started, you can find tips and support on websites such as www.smokefree.gov and the American Lung Association's www.lung.org/stop-smoking.

### Diet

Adopting healthy eating habits in your 50s is more important than ever in order to counteract changes that naturally occur with aging. For instance, both blood pressure and cholesterol levels tend to increase with age, so maintaining healthy ranges with diet and exercise is vital. When it comes to a healthy diet, there have been volumes written on the subject, with wide variations in advice. However, most experts agree that following a heart-healthy diet is your best bet. Eating a heart-healthy diet can lower blood pressure, reduce cholesterol, prevent diabetes, and keep weight in check. In fact, good eating habits are more effective against disease than medications.

You can ask your healthcare provider for healthy eating guidelines or find heart-healthy diets online on websites such as www.heart.org (The American Heart Association). In general, a heart-healthy diet includes:

- **Reducing sodium to prevent hypertension** (high blood pressure). Take the salt shaker off the table and check labels on prepared foods for sodium content—you might be surprised by what you find. Recommended guideline for sodium intake for healthy adults is 2,300 milligrams or less per day. However, older adults, African-Americans, and those with a diagnosis of hypertension should lower their daily intake to 1,500 milligrams or less. (On average, Americans consume double and even triple those amounts!)

- **Reducing saturated fats,** which are found in red meat, poultry skin, full-fat dairy products, butter, and cheese.
- **Avoiding trans fats,** which are artificial fats used to extend the shelf life of various packaged and processed foods, such as margarine, crackers, and bakery goods. Many deep fried and fast foods also contain trans fats.
- **Adding more "good" fats** (monounsaturated and polyunsaturated), which are found in foods such as avocados and nuts and some cooking oils (olive, canola, and sunflower).
- **Including omega-3 fatty acids** in your diet by eating fish, particularly deep-water, fatty fish (salmon, herring, trout, sardines, mackerel, and albacore tuna) at least two times per week.
- **Increasing fiber** with whole grain, high-fiber foods, such as whole grain breads and cereal, brown rice, couscous, quinoa, lentils, beans, nuts, oat bran, and oatmeal.
- **Avoiding refined flour products** and foods with added sugar (simple carbohydrates), such as white bread, cakes, cookies, sugar-added cereals, and soda pop. Beware of ingredients such as corn syrup, high-fructose corn syrup,

## To Supplement or Not

There is a dizzying array of vitamins, minerals, and other dietary supplements filling store shelves these days. There is also much debate in the medical community due to recent studies questioning the effectiveness of some supplements. And, the claims regarding these supplements can be confusing! While most experts agree that a good-quality multivitamin can help you fill in nutritional gaps, supplements are not meant to replace a balanced diet—eating a variety of natural foods is important for overall health. While it's always better to get nutrients naturally, there may be circumstances when a supplement is helpful, such as a diagnosed vitamin deficiency or health condition. The bottom line: Talk to your healthcare provider before taking any dietary supplements. Also, be sure to inform your healthcare provider of any supplements you have been taking, as certain supplements can interact adversely with prescription drugs, and others may cause complications with certain health conditions or surgery.

dextrose, and corn sweetener, among others, which are really sugar!

- **Loading up on fruits and vegetables** (five or more servings per day), which not only increase fiber, but provide essential nutrients. A diet high in fruit and vegetables has been linked to the prevention of certain types of cancer and lowers your risk for heart disease.

Encouragingly, studies show that when it comes to diet and exercise, even small changes can have big results. Conditions such as pre-diabetes, hypertension, and high cholesterol can often be improved or eliminated through diet and exercise, thus avoiding medications and worsening health.

### Exercise

As we age, we naturally lose muscle mass and bone density and tend to accumulate more fat. Perhaps you've noticed it's much more difficult to keep the weight off as you reach middle age, particularly around the middle! This type of stubborn weight gain is not only frustrating, it's also unhealthy. An expanding waistline signals an increase in visceral adiposity, a type of belly fat that negatively impacts cardiac health. This kind of fat has also been linked to poor glucose control (insulin resistance), which leads to type 2 diabetes, high blood pressure, and poor vascular health. Even if you're not considered overweight, it's possible to have more fat than is good for you.

Staying active and even stepping up your activity level can help combat this stubborn weight gain, while maintaining muscle mass and keeping bones strong. In fact, exercise can improve our quality of life as we age in many ways. All too often we assume that problems such as loss of strength, balance, and flexibility are just a natural consequence of getting older. However, research indicates that many of these issues are a result of years of inactivity, which means we can prevent them from occurring by staying active. What's more, regular exercise has been shown to improve cognitive function as we age, helping to stave off memory loss and dementia.

Exercise will not prevent every ailment that comes along as we get older, but it can enhance the aging process. The American Heart Association notes that for every hour of regular exercise you perform, you'll gain about two hours of additional life expectancy. More importantly, those added hours are likely to be healthier! So, how much and what type of exercise should you be doing?

Before beginning any exercise program, be sure to consult

your physician, especially if you've been sedentary. The type of exercise that's right for you will depend on your current physical condition, as well as the activities you enjoy—because you probably won't stick to something you don't like! It's also important to note that even those with disabilities or health problems can and should get regular exercise. If you're not sure where to start, consult with your healthcare provider or a physical therapist, who can tailor a program to fit your needs. In general, experts recommend:

- **At least 30 minutes or more** of moderate physical activity at least five days a week. Moderate-intensity exercise is defined as any activity that causes your heart rate and breathing pattern to noticeably increase—reaching approximately 50 to 70 percent of your maximum heart rate. For example, walking at a brisk pace for 30 minutes (approximately 4.0 mph), swimming laps for 20 minutes, and bicycling five miles in 30 minutes would be considered moderate activity. (See chapter 4 for heart rate calculations.)
- **Strength-building exercises** three times a week to maintain muscle mass and bone density. Examples of this type of exercise include using light weights,

resistance bands, or your own body weight as you perform abdominal crunches, bicep curls, push-ups, etc. In particular, improving core strength (abdominal muscles) can prevent back pain and improve mobility.

- **Exercises that improve balance and flexibility,** such as yoga and Pilates. Most injuries, including falls, are a result of loss in flexibility and balance.

No matter which activities you choose, the best way to reap the benefits of exercise is to make it a habit. Instead of thinking of exercise as a chore, try thinking of it as fun (or at least an investment in your future). Walking with a friend or trying a new activity can make exercise something to look forward to. (See chapter 3 for more creative ways to form the exercise habit.)

### Sexuality

According to surveys, older Americans are staying sexually active longer, and those in their 50s and 60s report being "very satisfied" with their sex lives. It makes sense when you consider that empty nesters typically have more time for each other and with maturity comes confidence. This can be the perfect time to reconnect with one another. However, there are some realities of aging that may affect sexuality, including:

- **Menopause**—As estrogen levels naturally decrease after menopause, some women may notice a decrease in their libido (sex drive). Low estrogen levels can also lead to decreased blood flow to the vagina, resulting in dryness that can make sexual intercourse uncomfortable or even painful. In addition, insomnia and mood swings may also negatively affect sexual function. Of course, every woman experiences menopause differently, so not all women report changes in sexuality during this time. If you do experience any of these problems, be sure to consult your healthcare provider. There are many ways to alleviate menopausal symptoms that affect sexuality.

- **Erectile dysfunction**—Commonly referred to as ED, this condition is the inability to achieve and sustain an erection more than 50 percent of the time. While it's often associated with getting older, ED is not considered normal for any age. Approximately 15 to 25 percent of men age 65 and older experience ED on a long-term basis, but in the majority of cases there is an underlying health issue to blame. Because the penis needs adequate blood flow to maintain an erection, common causes of ED include diseases that affect blood flow, such as athero-sclerosis (hardening of the arteries). Hypertension, high cholesterol, stress, depression, and certain medications can also cause ED. The first step is diagnosing the problem. Once diagnosed, there are many treatment options for ED. Your physician can help determine which treatment is right for your individual health profile.
- **Poor health**—Many conditions, such as hypertension, high cholesterol, diabetes, and heart disease, along with the medications used to treat these problems, can negatively impact sexual interest and performance for both men and women. Therefore, staying active, eating a healthy diet, and maintaining good health are the best things you can do for your love life!
- **Sexually transmitted diseases (STD)**—While pregnancy may no longer be of concern, it's important to remember to practice safe sex to avoid contracting an unwanted

STD. Unfortunately, as baby boomers are aging, statistics are showing an increase in STDs in that population. The old adage of "better safe than sorry" definitely applies here.

Since there is no reason not to remain sexually active throughout our lives, any problems you may experience should be discussed with your physician. We are sometimes embarrassed or hesitant to talk openly about these issues, but an honest discussion is the gateway to solving the problem. It's important to find a physician with whom you feel comfortable and can talk candidly. Communicating openly with your partner is also vital.

### Know Your Numbers

When is the last time you had a checkup? Do you know your cholesterol profile, blood pressure, and blood glucose level? These are important health indicators that everyone should know. Once you have these numbers, you can compare them to optimal ranges for men and women your age and determine if you need to make lifestyle changes. As importantly, you can track trends—blood pressure that is slowly creeping upward and an increase in LDL (bad) cholesterol are early warning signs. By catching them in a timely manner, you can often reverse these negative trends with diet and exercise, and avoid taking medications, which may cause side effects. However, if lifestyle changes are not enough to keep high cholesterol, hypertension, or pre-diabetes in check, medication should be considered (in conjunction with healthy habits). If you have already been diagnosed with a condition such as diabetes or high blood pressure, it's important to keep them under control in your 50s and avoid complications that may worsen with age.

In a word, preventative health screenings such as mammograms, colonoscopies, and prostate exams can be life-saving. These tests often detect diseases before you develop symptoms or in their earliest stages, when they are easier to treat. Which screenings you need and how often to have them performed will depend on your age, sex, family history, and whether you have risk factors for certain conditions. While most of us understand the benefits of early detection, many middle-aged and older Americans offer up a variety of reasons for not getting regular health screenings, including:

- I don't know which tests to get and how often.
- They are too expensive. / I don't have health insurance.
- They're not important unless you are sick.
- I don't have transportation.

To determine which tests you individually may need and when, consult with your physician. In fact, having regular checkups with a healthcare provider is the best way to monitor your health and schedule necessary screenings, as well as discuss the results and treatment options. Although tests can be expensive, many are offered at no cost under new healthcare laws. In addition, free or low-cost testing is typically offered at community centers, health fairs, and even drugstores. Also look for "traveling" health screenings that bring tests to senior housing communities, intended for those who may have limited transportation. With a national focus on preventative care, it's easier than ever to find resources for regular health screenings.

## The Sandwich Generation

According to the Pew Research Center, just over one of every eight Americans aged 40 to 60 is both raising a child and caring for an elderly parent, while one of every seven is providing financial support to both children and a parent. Of course, with the senior population expected to double by 2030, these numbers also continue to expand. This group is truly "sandwiched" between generations and, considering the added demands of both time and money, can certainly feel the squeeze.

"With an aging population and a generation of young adults struggling to achieve financial independence, the burden on middle-aged Americans is increasing," says Michael Johnson, CFP®, CPWA®. "It can be difficult enough to meet family obligations, pay your bills, and save for retirement without this additional pressure. If you expect to provide financial support for aging relatives or adult children, or both, you need to consider the impact this will have on your retirement plans." Johnson recommends consulting a financial expert, accountant, or estate planner to help you plan accordingly. There are often ways to adjust your investments to provide future income streams from dividends or annuities, as well as minimize taxes through trusts.

Though it can sometimes be a sensitive subject, it's also necessary to have a straightforward, compassionate conversation with aging parents, preferably before a long-term care situation arises. Together, conduct a financial inventory of your parents' income, assets, and insurance policies, including account numbers and passwords. At the same time, review their legal documents, including wills and powers of attorney. This is a good time to discuss their wishes regarding care and living options, along with the costs associated with those choices. Listen to their concerns and stay positive. After you've gathered the necessary information, organize it in a binder and store it in a secure location, such as a safe deposit box.

Once you have a complete picture of their financial situation, you might also be able to help your folks pare back expenses. Decisions such as selling the family home are often difficult for elderly parents, but downsizing could provide much-needed financial resources, as well as peace of mind. This is also the time to:

- **Discuss long-term care insurance.** If your parents are healthy enough to qualify, it could still be an option. The American Association for Long-Term Care Insurance (aaltci.org) can help you research possibilities, including purchasing your own policy. Remember, when it comes to long-term care insurance, the earlier you start to plan, the more options you have.
- **Investigate care alternatives,** such as adult day care. While it may seem more cost effective to quit your job to care for aging parents, be sure to consider the total

amount of income and benefits you will be sacrificing as compared to other care options. At $67 per day, on average, adult day care is much less than paid home care (approximately $21 per hour) and nursing homes (approximately $229 per day). Do your homework and assess all living/care options before making a decision.

- **Take advantage of tax breaks.** If your parent(s) live with you for more than half the year and you pay for adult day care or home care so you can work outside the home, you may be able to pay for those expenses with tax-free money. In some cases, you can contribute up to $5,000 per year to your employer's dependent care flexible spending account or claim the dependent care credit on your tax return.
- **Ask about caregiving benefits at work.** Some large companies offer elder-care service locators or other caregiving support as an employee benefit.
- **Find out if your parents are eligible** for federal, state, and other benefits through www.benefitscheckup.org.

Of course, financial support is only one aspect of the caregiving role. The additional demands on your time, as well as the emotional toll, can be challenging. American families provide 80 to 90 percent of all in-home long-term care for their loved ones, and many of these caregivers report feeling constantly stressed—another 31 percent always feel rushed or pressed for time. Feelings of guilt are also common—for not accomplishing all that "should" be done, even though they are doing all they can. It can be difficult to find balance: How do you split your time between children/family and elderly parents? How much time is too much as caregiver? What about your marriage and your own health? Unfortunately, there are no easy answers, but there are some things you can do to improve the situation:

- **Hold a family meeting.** Can caregiving duties be split among siblings or other family members? If so, it's important to create a detailed plan that everyone can agree upon. List daily and weekly tasks, along with who is responsible for each one. Be as specific as possible.
- **Keep communications open.** Everyone involved in the caregiving duties, including the recipient, should be informed about tasks, schedules, and changes in medical care. Likewise, those who may be affected by these responsibilities, such as your spouse and children, should be kept in the loop.
- **Ask for help.** There are numerous resources available for caregivers—if you look for them. Many caregivers feel like they must do everything themselves, but it's nearly impossible for one person to take on the roles of nurse, therapist, chauffeur, medical coordinator, and more without eventually suffering burnout. Don't be afraid to ask for help. A hospital social worker or physician can recommend resources. Family and friends may also be a good source of information or assistance. For example, asking each friend or family member who offers support for one specific piece of help (e.g., picking up prescriptions or delivering a meal) can really lighten your load. You can also contact your local Area Agency on Aging (National Association of Area Agencies on Aging at www.n4a.org.).
- **Take time to care for yourself.** Sure, this is easier said than done, but it's absolutely necessary. After all, you

can't take care of others if you don't take care of yourself. If you're sick, nothing will get done! To alleviate stress, be sure to schedule some regular "me time," even if it's just 10 to 20 minutes each day to do something you enjoy or simply relax. The same applies to your marriage: set aside time to connect without distractions. Finally, don't neglect your health—listen to your body, don't ignore symptoms, get regular checkups, continue to eat healthy meals, and exercise regularly.

- **Find support.** It's easy to get lost in the role of caregiver. Though caring for a loved one can be very rewarding, it can also be emotionally taxing. A quick Internet search reveals hundreds of caregiver support programs, both locally and nationally. These groups provide education, support, information, and referral services to people caring for loved ones. They can also offer an important outlet for the gamut of emotions many caregivers experience.

- **Focus on the positive.** Despite the stress, surveys reveal that most caregivers find caring for their loved ones gratifying. The experience can strengthen relationships and offer opportunities for personal growth. Research also shows that those who focus on the positive aspects of their role feel less burdened.

## Staying Vibrant

For many active, healthy 50-somethings, it's hard to imagine losing their spark. We may complain about the onset of aches and pains, or a certain lack of stamina, but otherwise feel good. And then something happens—it could be an injury or a health scare; it might be the loss of a loved one or a financial struggle. Suddenly we become aware of the emotional aspects of aging and the importance of staying mentally healthy. In fact, it's not uncommon for depression and anxiety to make an appearance as we reach midlife and beyond. How can you shore up your mental and emotional health? Over and over, research shows us that maintaining social ties and having a purpose-filled life are the most important factors in aging well. You can lay the groundwork by:

- **Staying active**—You need to be active during your midlife to remain lively in your late life. But, it's not just exercise that provides health benefits; hobbies such as gardening and cooking, which engage the body and mind and reduce stress levels, are also important.
- **Finding your spiritual side**—Cortisol, which is known as the stress hormone, can constrict blood vessels, rev up your heart rate, raise blood pressure, and increase blood sugar. Meditating or praying has been shown to significantly decrease cortisol levels. Engaging in spiritual practices also activates the vagus nerve, which slows your heartbeat and promotes calm.
- **Protecting your joints**—Are you starting to feel the first twinges of joint pain? It's time to get moving. A workout that combines low-impact cardio, strength training, and flexibility will protect joints, alleviate pain, and prevent further damage.
- **Forming social/community ties**—Being among friends is not only enjoyable, it's relaxing, which lowers blood pressure and boosts immunity. Instead of leaving encounters to chance, schedule regular standing dates with friends. You might also consider other social opportunities, such as joining a book club or volunteering in your community.

- **Continuing to learn**—Learning new things increases your cognitive reserves, which keeps your brain active for longer. Sign up for a class, try a new hobby, master another language, or brush up on your computer skills.
- **Living conscientiously**—It turns out that your mom's advice to "be good" and "play nice" was right! Longevity studies show that being thoughtful and conscientious leads to healthier behaviors and lifestyles, and contributes to your overall well-being.

Like Jan and her reaction to becoming an AARP member, we may find ourselves "surprised" to be considered seniors in our 50s. While it's great to feel and act younger than the years imply, it shouldn't prevent us from planning for the future. With a little preparation in our 50s, we can look forward to the coming decades—making them healthy, productive, and fulfilling.

## Words of Wisdom . . .

*Planning is important, but equally essential is the ability to adapt when things don't work out as intended. Instead of being derailed by life's unexpected twists and turns, those who age well find ways to get back on track.*

*"Sometimes I stop and wonder 'how did I get here?'" Skip mused. "As a young man, I would have never guessed that my career or my personal life would have taken the routes they have. But here I am, at 54, jumping into a new job and taking on new family responsibilities. In many ways, I'm the happiest I've ever been."*

*Early on, Skip thought he was destined to be in the food business. His parents were grocers in the 1970s, and it seemed natural to join the family enterprise. When the economy forced them to sell the supermarket, he became a sales representative in the food industry, where he had developed a long list of contacts. One day, however, a friend suggested that his considerable people skills would be perfect for the publishing business—something he had never considered. Before long he was working for that friend as a book editor, which eventually led Skip and several colleagues to launch their own publishing company.*

*"It was an interesting venture, but over time we discovered we had very different opinions about the company's direction," recalled Skip. "We sold the business and went our separate ways. Sometimes things work out, and sometimes they don't, but every experience is an opportunity to learn and grow."*

*After pursuing careers in printing and later in electronic resource sales, Skip decided to take a leap and invest his energy in a young start-up venture. It's not what he expected at this point in his life, but he's been energized by the prospects of something new. Of course, career paths are not the only thing subject to change.*

*"At the age of 50, I unexpectedly found myself divorced after 27 years of marriage," said Skip. "It was definitely a low point in my life, because it felt like a failure. In hindsight, you think of all the things you would have done differently, but you can't change the past. You have to learn from the experience, pick up the pieces, and move on."*

*Following the divorce, Skip was in no hurry to start dating, but sometimes love finds you when you're not looking for it. He met his second wife at work and suddenly understood what people meant when they referred to "love at first sight." The relationship was not without trials, however; there was the matter of blending Skip's two adult children with his new wife's teenage daughters, one of whom is autistic.*

*"Caring for a stepdaughter with special needs, as well as helping kids who are still struggling through school and trying to find their way, has been challenging, but also very rewarding," Skip confessed. "When my kids were young, I remember thinking that things would get easier as they got older, but being a parent doesn't get easier, it just changes during different stages. And now we have aging parents to consider, so there are new responsibilities added to the mix."*

*Through all the changes in Skip's life, one thing has remained constant: his love of sports. A lifelong athlete, Skip has remained active, running and cycling, playing soccer, basketball and softball as an adult, and participating in triathlons. He hopes to complete a marathon this year. Aside from the obvious health benefits, Skip credits his active lifestyle for reducing stress and helping him maintain a positive outlook—something that becomes more important with age.*

*"In recent years, I've lost two friends to cancer and watched my parents struggle with some health issues," said Skip. "It's given me a keener sense of how fleeting life is and how important it is to live life to the fullest. I've become more mindful of how I live—more charitable, more generous to my family and friends, and packing more into my days. You don't know what the future holds, so you need to make the most of the present. I tell my kids that a little savings goes a long way—not just financial savings, but other 'deposits' you make along the way, like the way you treat other people, taking care of your health, giving back to the community, doing things you love—it all begins to mean more as you get older."*

# CHAPTER THREE

# Building on Experience: Your 60s

*"Aging is not lost youth, but a new stage
of opportunity and strength."*
—BETTY FRIEDAN

## Snowbirds

*Less than a year after Bill and Diane retired, they had sold their suburban home and moved to a condominium in Florida. Weary of the long Midwest winters and ready for a change, they did what a large number of Americans do each year—flock south.*

*"At first it was lovely," recalled Diane. "The warm weather and sunshine were so welcome."*

*But the novelty soon began to wear off. The couple's two grown children and three young grandchildren were now far away, and Diane found herself missing their once-frequent visits, as well as occasional babysitting duties. She realized her grandchildren would only be little for a short while, and it pained her to miss spending time with them during this precious age.*

*"When we moved, we imagined the kids coming down to stay with us," said Bill. "But with busy jobs, the kids' activities, and expenses, they just can't get away very often."*

*Both Bill and Diane also missed their social connections in Illinois. Diane had been active in their church, and Bill played golf regularly with a group of friends. Though they tried joining some clubs down south, they found themselves "doing nothing" for much of the time.*

*"Looking back, I realize we didn't think things through before we moved," admitted Diane. "It just seemed like the thing to do. We know people who love it down south, but it wasn't for us. Doing nothing is nice for a vacation, but not long term. I could feel myself getting older by the minute!"*

*Within three years, they had moved back to Illinois, finding a small condo close to their daughter and her family and within a four-hour drive of their son. The condo happens to be in a naturally occurring retirement community (NORC), which means that most of the residents are seniors. Between visits with the kids, babysitting, volunteer work, spending time with the old gang, and socializing with their new neighbors, they are busier than ever. Bill even decided to go back to work part-time at the local golf shop. They are still not fans of the long winters but have compromised by renting a place in Florida for the months of January and February each year. For this couple, home is where their family and friends are!*

Bill and Diane's story is a common one. As their experience illustrates, there is no cookie-cutter retirement plan; what works for some people may not be right for others. It also demonstrates the need for planning.

## A Time of Change—Or Not

Attitudes toward retirement have changed considerably over the years. In 1950, the average man retiring at the age of 65 could expect to live another 13 years (women another 15). Today, the average man and woman can look forward to 17 to 20 more years, respectively, but many people live much longer. And because we are staying healthier into our late years, the traditional age and meaning of retirement have also evolved. While a good number of people are ready to "retire" in their mid-60s, trends indicate that older adults are increasingly interested in ways to stay busy and remain productive, whether through a new career, part-time employment opportunities, or volunteer activities.

For instance, though retirement rates rise steeply at 62 and 65 (the ages of Social Security eligibility), many people remain in the workforce either full- or part-time. According to a 2002 poll, 50 percent of those 65 and older were working part-time, and, surprisingly, 10 percent of those 84 years old had part-time jobs! Of those aged 65–69 who were still working, 30 percent were self-employed. When asked, baby boomers said they expect to work longer than previous generations. The reasons vary. For some, the structure and availability of pensions strongly influence their decision about when to give up work. Health problems can also have a big impact on retirement plans. However, more often than not, people simply want to feel useful.

Sociologists point to a number of factors influencing our changing attitudes toward retirement, including the fact that jobs have become less labor intensive, allowing people to work longer. In some cases, the decision to delay retirement is driven by economic necessity—a trend that appears to be growing. People are also more willing to change careers and try something new. In fact, over 80 percent of those 60 to 69 years old indicate a desire to "do something different," instead of leaving the workforce entirely.

## New Directions

Many folks consider this a time to begin their "second act"—an opportunity to do something they've always wanted to do or explore new interests. Given the choice, a large number of people would like to combine a passion with a paycheck, like Ted.

*Ted retired from his sales job when he was 62. After years in a high-pressure career that often involved travel, he had new goals that included spending more time with his family, having a more flexible schedule, and giving back to the community. He parlayed his people skills and sales experience into a new job raising funds for a local charity—one that he had worked with in the past and held a special place in his heart.*

*In his new position as a professional fundraiser, Ted organizes events, lines up speakers, and spends a lot of time on the phone drumming up donations, which can all be done from his home office. The hours vary, but even during the busiest periods, he estimates that he works less than 30 hours per week. Of course, his paycheck is substantially less than "preretirement," but he describes his job as "extremely satisfying."*

Ted represents a new generation of 60-somethings who are reinventing themselves and finding fulfillment in a second career. This is good news, because, as we've seen, living a purpose-filled life can help us age well.

However, before you begin your second act, it's a good idea to outline the script! Along with your spouse and/or other family

### Life Reimagined

A new personalized program offered by AARP, Life Reimagined, is designed to help people explore new life choices using a multimedia set of tools and resources. It includes an online assessment tool and activities that lead you through the six steps of positive change: reflect, connect, explore, choose, repack, and act. The program also covers themes such as purpose, passion, and the power of experiences and shares inspiring stories of people who revitalized their lives. "It's possible—and in fact, it's necessary—for people to continue to change and evolve, no matter how old they are," says Bill Thomas, M.D., fellow for The Life Reimagined Institute for Innovation. To begin your personal reinvention, visit LifeReimagined.org.

members, take the time to talk about how you envision the future, what goals you would like to accomplish, and what your priorities are. Some important questions to consider include:

- **Are you social or solitary?** Are your social connections or community ties important to your happiness and well-being? If so, severing these ties could be detrimental to your mental and physical health.
- **How much time do you and your spouse want to spend together on a daily basis?** How much is too much? Do you both have separate interests or hobbies?
- **Do you want to be close to family members?** If you are currently spending a lot of time visiting or babysitting, moving far away will mean a major change. Don't rely on children, who may be busy with careers and young families, to travel long distances to visit frequently.
- **Does your current residence require a lot of maintenance?** Are you physically capable of doing that work? Will you be physically capable in 5 to 10 years? Can you afford to hire services such as lawn care, snow removal, etc.? If you plan on traveling, does your current residence allow you to leave for an extended period of time without worry?
- **Does downsizing make financial sense?** If so, what type of community appeals to you—a small town with shops and restaurants within walking distance, a maintenance-free condo complex, a retirement village with amenities? Have you researched these options?
- **What is your current health status (honest assessment)?** What about the next 5 to 10 years? Are you having trouble with stairs or experiencing other mobility

problems? If so, these issues should be factored into your choice of living arrangements.

- **What is really important to you?** Make a list of priorities (i.e., time for travel, proximity to family, volunteer work) and then look for living arrangements that fit your list.

## More Than a Move

*Joan and Steve had been thinking about moving to an independent living community for quite some time. Mobility issues were making the stairs difficult for Steve, and the upkeep on their home was becoming too much to handle both physically and financially. The idea of downsizing and relinquishing some responsibility was appealing, but the thought of actually sorting through and packing up a lifetime of memories was overwhelming.*

*"Sometimes I would walk from room to room and think 'what will we do with all this stuff?" admitted Joan. "We don't have a lot of expensive heirlooms or antiques, but so many things have sentimental value, like the big pine table in our dining room. Every nick and ding reminds me of all the family gatherings and holidays we've celebrated around that table. I know we can't take everything with us, but how do you part with the things you cherish?"*

*Seeing her parents struggle with the decision to move, the couple's oldest daughter decided to seek some professional advice.*

Whether you are making a decision to downsize or helping your parents move, the task can be daunting. In fact, surveys indicate that the thought of downsizing can be so paralyzing it prevents many seniors from making a move that would be beneficial. Often, the biggest question is where to start? Fortunately, there are now a growing number of companies that specialize in downsizing and moving seniors that can help make the process manageable.

"There are many issues to overcome," says Bryan Neal, Senior Move Manager, Assisted Moving LLC. "But, like many large tasks, it becomes easier when you break it down into smaller steps. Since every situation is unique, we always begin by taking the time to find out what's really important to the people moving, what the concerns are, and how other family members are involved in the process."

Next, Neal recommends making an inventory and sorting belongings into four categories: keep, pass on to others, donate/sell, and discard. Communication among family members is very important during this stage. Many seniors assume their adult children will willingly inherit many of the items they will need to leave behind. Unfortunately, this is not always the case. Adult children often don't have the space for or interest in receiving some possessions. Making a list of family members who have specified an interest in particular items prior to a move is a good way to pass items on when the time comes. In addition, many companies can help you organize an estate sale, sell items on consignment, or arrange for donations. And, when it comes to adjusting to a smaller space, professional organizers can help you make the most of the situation.

It's important to note that in many cases, this type of move can be emotionally charged for both seniors and their adult children. While children may be concerned about their parents' safety or lack of companionship, it's not uncommon for many seniors to resist the idea of moving from their life-long home. They might be unaware of or underestimate their decreased physical abilities, as well as fearful of losing their independence or parting with cherished memorabilia. Psychologically, downsizing can be akin to loss and should be handled with compassion.

"This is more than just a move," cautions Neal. "Sometimes an unbiased third-party professional can ease the anxiety and facilitate communication between seniors and concerned children. We have the expertise to help seniors make difficult decisions and create a strategy. I have seen many instances where once a plan is in place, and everyone can visualize that plan, both seniors and their families feel better and can move forward. More often than not, people come back to thank us and tell us the move was a good decision."

*Working with professionals and creating a manageable plan helped Joan and Steve finally make their move. Certain "must haves" such as Steve's favorite chair and Joan's refurbished desk fit nicely into their new apartment. Some possessions found new homes with the couple's children, while others were donated. The pine table, which was too big for either of the children's homes, was sold to a young couple who fell in love with its warmly worn surface and would surely create new memories around it. While it was still difficult to part with some of their treasured belongings, Joan and Steve were excited to begin a new chapter in their lives.*

*"Once the details were handled, I felt like a huge weight was lifted and I began to look forward to a fresh start," Joan acknowledged. "Besides, it gave me a good excuse to finally buy a new couch!" she added with a grin.*

Assisted Moving LLC is a professional downsizing and moving service designed specifically for senior citizens and their families who are relocating to or from a senior community. The company is located in Plymouth, Michigan.

## Best Laid Plans

If you're fit and healthy at this stage in your life, you may not be thinking about losing your mobility or being able to keep up with yard work and home maintenance, but change is inevitable, and often the best laid plans are derailed by unexpected circumstances. While it's impossible to predict the future or plan for every scenario, you can still be proactive. For example, when downsizing, it's wise to choose a single-level home or condo, even if stairs are not currently an issue. Likewise, finding a place with wider hallways that could accommodate a walker or wheelchair if that becomes necessary is sensible. Many new retirement communities are designed with these possibilities in mind. They offer easy-to-navigate layouts, eliminate thresholds that may cause trips and falls, install safety bars in tubs and showers, lower cabinets and shelves for easier reach, and more. If you are planning to stay in your home or condo for many years, it makes sense to anticipate future needs.

## Money Matters

When making a decision to retire, either completely or partially, the first step is to assess your financial situation. This is best done with the help of a financial advisor, who can inventory your current assets and plot a personalized course for the future. Investments may need to be adjusted at this stage in the game to further reduce risk and focus on income. At retirement age, there are other considerations to make, such as:

- **As mentioned, age 59½** is the first age at which you can begin taking withdrawals from traditional IRA accounts and some qualified retirement plans without a penalty tax, but you're not required to take distributions until age 70½.
- **At age 62,** you can begin receiving Social Security benefits, but you'll receive more if you wait until your full retirement age, which varies (see below). Also, if you continue to work, Social Security benefits will be

reduced by $1 for every $2 in earnings.

- **Somewhere between the age 65 and 67** you are eligible to receive 100 percent of your Social Security benefits. The age varies, depending on birth year. For example, individuals born in 1955 are eligible to receive 100 percent of their benefits when they reach 66 years and two months. Those born in 1960 or later must reach age 67 before they are eligible to receive full benefits. (Keep in mind, these eligibility ages are currently the subject of much debate and could change.)

- **At age 65,** you can also enroll in Medicare and Medicare Part B (see "Making Sense of Medicare and Medicaid" for more information). If you are already receiving Social Security benefits, you will be automatically enrolled in Medicare Part A (hospitalization) and Part B (medical insurance). If you are not receiving Social Security benefits yet, it's recommended that you apply for Medicare three months before reaching age 65.

## Making Sense of Medicare and Medicaid

Both Medicare and Medicaid are governmental programs that provide medical and health-related services to specific groups of people in the United States. However, the two programs are very different. **Medicaid** provides coverage for certain individuals and families with low incomes and few resources. Although this program is overseen at the federal level, each state establishes its own eligibility requirements and determines the type, amount, duration, and scope of services. Though Medicaid programs differ in each state, there are some mandatory federal requirements that must be met in order for the state to receive federal matching funds. These required services include inpatient hospital stays, outpatient hospital services, prenatal care, vaccines for children, physician services, and more. To determine if you are eligible for Medicaid, you can visit www.healthcare.gov/do-i-qualify/. If you do qualify for Medicaid benefits, it's important to research the program specific to the state in which you live. Some state-specific programs offer additional long-term support and in-home services (sometimes known as Medicaid Waivers).

**Medicare** is a federal health insurance program that provides medical coverage for seniors age 65 and older and certain disabled Americans. You become eligible for Medicare benefits on your 65th birthday (you should apply for benefits three months prior), and those who receive Social Security are automatically enrolled in the basic plan (parts A and B). There are several categories of Medicare coverage:

**Part A:** Provides coverage for hospital care, limited nursing home stays, hospice, and some home healthcare. Most people who have been employed receive Part A coverage without having to pay a monthly premium.

**Part B:** Provides supplementary coverage, such as physician visits, outpatient services, and some medical equipment. Many seniors purchase this additional coverage, which involves a monthly premium plus co-pays (typically 20 percent). Once you qualify for Medicare, enrollment in Part B is usually automatic.

**Part C:** Sometimes referred to as Medicare Advantage, Part C plans are purchased through insurance companies and provide more comprehensive medical coverage. Some plans may include coverage for prescription drugs, dental visits, vision care, and even contributions toward gym memberships, diet-related programs, and more. Medicare Advantage programs include all Part A and Part B coverage, so you don't need the two base plans if you have a Medicare Advantage policy. Monthly premiums vary by the insurance carrier and specific plan.

**Part D:** Also known as a prescription drug plan, these policies pay for outpatient prescription and generic drug coverage. If you don't sign up immediately for one of these plans when you reach age 65, you face penalties for joining later.

**AB+ or Medigap:** This is a supplemental policy offered by private insurers that adds to coverage under Parts A and B.

Each year, from October through early December, there is an enrollment period for Medicare, which allows individuals to review their plans and change their options. Because the terminology, parts, and plans can be confusing, it's helpful to attend free informational meetings held within your community or work with a plan coordinator. The Area Agency on Aging Medicare/Medicaid Assistance Program has local agencies around the country and typically holds meetings during the annual enrollment period. When it comes to determining which Part D (prescription) program is right for you, your local pharmacy can be a valuable resource.

### A New Focus

With more than 9,000 Americans turning 65 each day, seniors enrolling in Medicare represent a strong market force. This demand, coupled with a new focus on preventative care, has led to an expansion in the type of services provided through Medicare programs. Today, you are more likely to receive reminders for scheduling regular lab tests or getting your flu shot. In addition, extra efforts are being made to involve family members in a patient's care and provide follow-up visits from social workers or nurses after a senior patient leaves the hospital. In fact, over recent years, Medicare has begun to cover screenings for depression, obesity, sexually transmitted diseases, and alcohol/drug misuse. This new focus follows the trend of healthcare providers directing more of their efforts on keeping healthy patients healthy and helping chronically ill patients take better control of their diseases.

In some states, new programs are emerging to help Medicare recipients manage their medical coverage, particularly for those who qualify for both Medicare and Medicaid. These "dual eligibles" often have multiple medical conditions, see several specialists and, as a result, are overwhelmed with the paperwork involved in managing their coverage. These programs assign Care Coordinators to help patients make and keep scheduled appointments, communicate with providers, sort out paperwork, and answer questions.

When trying to determine the best Medicare plans for you, the first thing you should consider is your individual health. The best policy for one person may not be optimal for another. Be sure to consider all the options before signing up for a particular program. For more information, you can access the following resources:

**www.medicare.gov**—Go to "find health and drug plans," which allows you to narrow your choices by using your ZIP code, medications, or even preferred pharmacy.

**Medicare hot line at 800.MEDICARE (800.633.4227)** —A counselor can help you search for options over the phone and mail you a summary.

**"Medicare and You"**—This brochure is typically sent to potential beneficiaries at age 65. If you don't receive a copy, you can request one

This is also a good time to evaluate your need for long-term care (LTC) insurance. According to the 2014 National Medicare Handbook (*Medicare & You*), at least 70 percent of people over age 65 will need some type of long-term care services during their lifetime—services that can be very expensive and the costs continue to rise. Many underestimate the costs associated with long-term care or incorrectly assume Medicare or other health insurance will provide coverage. They may not. In fact, Medicare will only pay for this type of care for a short time and under limited circumstances. More importantly, in-home care, which is the most preferred type of care, is not covered at all. LTC insurance gives you the freedom to choose what type of care you receive and where you receive it, while protecting your loved ones from the cost burden.

In general, the younger and healthier you are the more coverage options you have and the more affordable those options are. Certain preexisting conditions may prevent you from obtaining LTC insurance. For instance, if you already require assistance with activities of daily living (ADLs) such as bathing or dressing, or you've been diagnosed with a progressive condition, you may not be eligible. No one plans on suffering a stroke, developing a debilitating illness, or having an accident, but sadly, it happens every day. And after it happens, it's too late to obtain coverage.

Consulting with an insurance professional is your best bet,

but you can also visit the National Advisory Center for Long-Term Care Insurance (longtermcareinsurance.org). This site includes a cost calculator to help you determine average costs of care in your area and how much you will need to save or insure against, as well as answers to commonly asked questions and free quotes. One good question to ask is what happens if I cannot afford to pay the premiums after retirement—will I lose coverage completely? Keep in mind that every LTC insurance company has different parameters, which can vary from state to state. It's also important to consider adding a home care addendum or assisted living addendum to your policy if this is the type of care you would prefer. In other words, be sure to research all the options before purchasing a policy and be specific about the types of coverage it offers.

## Legal Issues

If you haven't already put your estate in order, including the creation of a living will and healthcare proxy, it's time. (See chapter 2 "Legal Issues" for more on this topic.) Again, while there are many online resources available to help you create these important documents, an attorney who specializes in estate planning or elder law is recommended to guide you through the process. Be sure your spouse, adult children, or other family members who might be caregivers are familiar with these documents—all parties should have a copy, know where the originals are located, and have discussed the details with you. Reviewing these documents every year or so, as things change, is also advised.

"We do a good job planning for many things in life, such as weddings, births, and graduations, but when it comes to end-of-life issues, many people leave it to chance," says Christopher

J. Berry, Certified Elder Law Attorney. "It may not be pleasant to think about, but having your affairs in order is really a gift for your loved ones. The last thing a grieving spouse or other family member needs is to struggle with legalities or difficult decisions. Most of my clients feel a sense of relief and say they have greater peace of mind once they complete the planning process. The hardest part seems to be getting started."

## Health Factors

Like it or not, our bodies change as we age: blood pressure creeps upward, LDL (bad) cholesterol tends to rise, and blood glucose levels increase. We also lose muscle mass and bone density over the years. To counteract these negative changes, it becomes even more important to eat a healthy diet and exercise regularly. In fact, as Dave learned, lifestyle choices can help you beat the odds.

*As an insurance adjustor, Dave knows a lot about risk assessment, so when his physician told him that his strong family history put him at an increased risk for heart disease, he decided to manage that threat. Physicians define a family history of premature heart disease as having a first-degree female relative (mother, sister, or daughter) under the age of 65 or a first-degree male relative (father, brother, or son) under the age of 55 with heart disease. Since Dave's father and grandfather both suffered from premature heart disease, his risk was increased, but developing the problem was not inevitable. As his doctor explained, there are many risk factors for heart disease, including age, gender, family history, hypertension, cholesterol levels, diabetes, smoking, excess weight, and sedentary lifestyle.*

*"I can't change my gender, my age, or my genes, but I decided to take control of the things I could," said Dave. "Knowing I was at an increased risk for heart disease made me more aware of my health. I eat a heart-healthy*

*diet—at least most of the time—and try to exercise regularly. My wife also makes sure I get an annual checkup."*

*In addition to his healthy habits, Dave learned that physicians use tools such as the Framington Risk Score (www.framingtonheartstudy.org/risk) and Reynolds Risk Score (www.reynoldsriskscore.org) to assess a patient's probability of developing heart disease and determine how aggressively to treat those risk factors. A natural number cruncher, Dave went online armed with the test results from his most recent physical to determine his own risk score. His age (65) and gender increased his risk a bit, but his total cholesterol of 185 mg/dL and HDL (good) cholesterol level of 50 mg/dL worked in his favor. A slightly elevated systolic blood pressure of 140 bumped up his risk, but his status as a non-smoker was a big plus. Overall, the Framington calculator put his 10-year risk of developing heart disease at 12 percent, while the Reynolds risk tool (which factors in family history) assessed his risk at 23 percent. Both percentages put him in the low to intermediate range—though not ideal, it was much better than he expected.*

*Encouraged by this news, Dave decided that rather than letting genes dictate his destiny, he would step up his efforts to protect his heart. Since Dave was already following a heart-healthy diet, his physician recommended that he reduce his sodium intake even further and increase his activity level to bring down his blood pressure and keep cholesterol levels in check. Adding omega-3 to his diet, either by eating more fatty fish or taking a supplement or both, was also recommended.*

### Diet and Exercise

As we discussed in the last chapter, following a heart-healthy diet and exercising regularly are the most powerful defenses against many health issues, especially heart disease. If your blood pressure is trending upward, like Dave's, you need to reduce your sodium intake. If your LDL (bad) cholesterol is on

Did you know? Statistics show that by the age of 65, half of all American men and a third of all American women are likely to suffer from heart disease—the leading cause of death for both sexes. The best treatment for heart disease is prevention through lifestyle choices. Visit www.framingtonheartstudy.org/risk to assess your 10-year risk.

the rise, while HDL (good) cholesterol is declining, dietary changes are in order. And, if these numbers put you in a high-risk category, it may also be time to consider medication to lower cholesterol or control your blood pressure. Keep in mind, however, that medication is more effective when combined with lifestyle changes.

In addition to dietary changes, exercise can also reduce blood pressure and cholesterol levels, as well as keeping you fit. Unless you've been very active, running a marathon or other intense exercise routines are not necessary—bouts of moderate activity on a regular basis are just as effective. The American Heart Association recommends at least 30 minutes of moderate physical activity, five days a week, which can be broken up into 10-minute stretches. For example, a brisk 10-minute walk in the morning combined with 20 minutes of bike riding in the evening meets the minimum requirements.

It bears repeating that many of the problems we associate with aging, such as falling and having difficulty getting out of a chair or car, are the result of losing strength, balance, and flexibility due to inactivity. That means we can prevent, or at least slow down, a good number of mobility problems by staying active. Even cognitive function can be improved with regular exercise.

It's never too late to start the exercise habit, but if you have not been active, you should consult a physician before beginning any exercise routine. Even those folks with cardiac problems or disabilities can and should benefit from regular exercise that is tailored to their conditions.

Need more motivation to get moving? Consider the following benefits of regular exercise:

- **Weight control**—Regular physical activity reduces the likelihood of becoming overweight or obese, which can lead to type 2 diabetes, hypertension, and other potential health problems.
- **Lower blood pressure**—Staying active can lower blood pressure from 5 to 15 mmHg, which can mean the difference between having to take medication for hypertension or not. If you are taking medication to control your blood pressure, exercising will boost the benefits of your prescription and may reduce the need for it altogether.
- **Improved cholesterol levels**—Regular exercise can keep LDL cholesterol and harmful triglycerides in check, as well as increase levels of heart-healthy HDL cholesterol. Again, exercise can mean the difference between having to take cholesterol-lowering medications or not. If you are already taking medication, exercise can improve the results.
- **Regulate blood sugar**—Exercise improves your body's ability to regulate blood sugar because increasing muscle mass and decreasing fat help your body to use insulin more effectively. If you have a family history of diabetes, preventing insulin resistance through exercise becomes even more important. Studies show that lifestyle factors, including diet and exercise, are actually more effective than prescription medication in the prevention of type 2 diabetes.
- **Reduced inflammation**—Inflammation in the body has

# Exercising Can Be Fun, Really!

You're more likely to stick with an exercise habit if it's something you enjoy, instead of a chore. For some, the thought of walking on a treadmill every day or joining a gym is simply unappealing. So, why not make exercise fun? With a little creativity, you can combine exercise with learning a new skill or social occasions. In fact, pairing exercise with social interaction provides two healthy benefits, as well as making it harder to skip! Here are few suggestions to get you started:

**Start a walking club**—Walking can be a great time to catch up with friends, while staying fit. Setting a regular time with a pal or group of neighbors will help keep you motivated and give you something to look forward to.

**Learn something new**—Have you always wanted to try ballroom dancing? Grab your spouse, a friend, or sign up for lessons on your own. Dancing is great exercise and music is a proven stress reliever. Plus, learning a new skill improves cognitive function! If dancing is not your speed, why not sign up for a yoga, Pilates, or water aerobics class? Don't be afraid that you won't get the hang of it. There are classes available at every level and for every age group. Check your local community center for a list of offerings.

**Get outside**—Studies show that exercising outside not only improves your mood, you're more likely to exercise longer when outdoors. Take a nature hike, walk the dog, throw the football around with the kids or grandkids, find a scenic bike trail and head out for an afternoon adventure. Even chores such as raking leaves and mowing the lawn count toward your daily activity level.

**Be sneaky**—Find ways to squeeze exercise into your daily routine. Park your car farther from the entrance to stores and walk. Use the stairs, if you are able, instead of the elevator. Get up from your desk every hour for a five- to ten-minute stroll. Bring your gym shoes for a lunchtime walk. Dance to one of your favorite songs in the middle of the day. Do a set of leg lifts or curl ups during the commercial break while watching television. Chase the grandkids around in a game of hide-and-seek. The possibilities are endless.

been linked to premature heart disease. However, regular physical activity reduces inflammation and lowers levels of C-reactive protein (a marker for inflammation).

- **Stress reduction**—Exercise stimulates chemicals in the brain that leave you feeling more relaxed and happier. Studies also show that regular exercise reduces anxiety and stress and can even lessen the symptoms of depression.
- **A stronger heart**—The heart is a muscle and, like all muscles, it needs regular exercise to keep it fit. When a heart gets weak due to inactivity, it pumps less blood with each beat, reducing circulation and causing the heart to beat more often to keep up. In contrast, a fit heart beats stronger and slower, producing a more robust circulation and keeping artery walls in good condition.

### Sexuality

As we've discussed, greater longevity and improved health are allowing seniors to stay sexually active throughout their lives. In fact, government agency statistics show that people over 60 are now the fastest growing group contracting sexually transmitted diseases. Why the increase? Unfortunately, higher divorce rates and the loss of spouses mean there is a large number of single people in this age group, and thanks to Internet dating sites (some tailored to seniors), starting new relationships is easier than ever. After menopause there is no longer a fear of pregnancy, so some may be forgoing safe sex. Older folks may also be reluctant to talk openly about these issues. However, all age groups are susceptible to sexually transmitted diseases and should take precautions.

The good news is intimacy benefits from having more time together and not worrying about childcare duties or job stress.

And though menopause can cause issues such as waning desire, many post-menopausal women report quicker arousal and more satisfaction with their sex lives. Perhaps some of this has to do with greater self-confidence (i.e., fewer hang-ups about our bodies) and less fear. Seniors are also expressing a more positive attitude about the aging process—we don't feel old!

Of course, sexuality can be hampered by health problems as we age. Cardiovascular issues can make some fearful of sexual activity. Diabetes can change hormone levels that affect desire. Arthritis and other painful conditions can make intimacy difficult. And, medications can reduce interest and cause erectile dysfunction. In fact, most erectile dysfunction stems from underlying health issues such as poor circulation, hypertension, or high cholesterol, as well as the medications used to treat these problems.

The best thing you can do to improve this aspect of your life is to take good care of your health, including keeping your weight in check, eating well, and staying active. Regular exercise can give your libido a boost in many ways, including better muscle tone and flexibility, increased stamina, and greater self-image. In addition, the chemicals released during exercise enhance our mood, which contributes to sexual desire. Exercise can also improve conditions such as diabetes and hypertension, which may negatively impact sexuality.

The key to having a fulfilling sexual relationship as we grow older is recognizing how the aging process can affect our body and work with those changes. We shouldn't be afraid to talk about these issues with our physicians, who can often help alleviate problems, as well as our partners. Keeping communication open can be difficult if we're not accustomed to discussing sexual issues (a common problem for seniors), but it's necessary for intimacy. The sexuality you experience in your late life may be different than what you enjoyed in your early life, but for many, it can be just as fulfilling.

> ## To Stay Healthy, 60-Somethings Should
> - Continue following a heart-healthy diet and exercising regularly.
> - Reduce sodium intake to less than 2,000 mg per day (less than 1,500 mg, if possible, particularly if you have been diagnosed with hypertension).
> - Have an annual physical exam and schedule any necessary health screenings.
> - Know your numbers—have blood pressure checked annually. If you have been diagnosed with high blood pressure and are taking medication, home monitoring may be advised. Have cholesterol and blood glucose levels checked every two to five years, depending on your personal risk factors. If these numbers are elevated, tests should be performed more frequently.
> - Take all medications as directed—never discontinue or change medication schedules without consulting your physician.

## Staying Vibrant

Data from the Health and Retirement Study (HRS), in conjunction with the University of Michigan, show that most people are happy and active in retirement—61 percent of retirees surveyed say they found the transition very satisfying. One-third noted moderate satisfaction, and only 7 percent reported dissatisfaction. Over and over, we find the key to being satisfied and staying vibrant is living with purpose.

More than ever, this generation of 60-somethings is leading active, fulfilling lives, which may include second careers, volunteer work, interesting new hobbies, travel, and time with family. The type of activities you pursue is not as important as the meaning it imparts. As long as you engage in the things you find meaningful, you can add years to your life—and life to your years! (See chapters 2 and 4 "Staying Vibrant" for tips on remaining active and mentally sharp.)

### Reasons to Retire

Among folks ages 60 to 69, the number one reason for retiring is "to spend more time with family," followed by (2) wanting to do other things; (3) poor health; and (4) didn't like work. What will your reason be?

## Words of Wisdom . . .

When Dorothy and her husband Jim decided to retire in their early 60s, it was not a decision they took lightly.

"Jim was an accountant, so the decision-making process involved a lot of spreadsheets and graphs," quipped Dorothy. "I may tease him about that, but the truth is it takes planning to retire well. Assessing your finances, making projections, and deciding what you really want in retirement are important considerations. We debated for quite a while and then finally decided to take the leap."

Planning is something that Dorothy and her husband do well. They started saving for retirement early on and, according to Dorothy, "lived a pretty frugal lifestyle" while raising four children and putting them through college. In addition, two of their children have type 1 diabetes, which required a strict schedule of testing and injections, along with proper meal planning. Their oldest daughter, who developed the autoimmune condition when she was 9 years old, eventually required both kidney and pancreatic transplants. Those were difficult times for the family, but now as they enjoy spending time with 11 grandchildren, ages 7 to 19, they count their blessings daily. They are also finding time to pursue some passions.

"We couldn't do much traveling when the kids were young," said Dorothy. "But now we're making up for it! We've been all over Europe and the Mediterranean, and this year we're planning a New England cruise. Every year, we escape the winter by spending a month in Florida. I think the key to retirement is finding balance. Like most people, we can't do everything, so we focus on the things we enjoy most."

At 69, Dorothy also recognizes that being healthy is essential to making the most of their retirement. She feels fortunate to be in good health and credits her active lifestyle. When she was approaching her 60th birthday, her daughter urged her to walk a 26.2 mile marathon for the American Heart Association. Though hesitant, she completed that marathon and got hooked.

Since then, Dorothy has participated in several half marathons and 5K events. Additionally, she has been walking three days a week with a regular group of friends for the past six years. She admits that some days she needs a little prodding, but having the support of a group makes it easier to stay on track.

"When you have a regular commitment, it motivates you to keep walking because you don't want to let anyone down," advised Dorothy. "Not only has walking helped me to lose weight and stay fit, it's also a great stress reliever."

Besides walking, Dorothy and Jim enjoy bike riding regularly. For them, being outdoors is more enjoyable than working out in a gym, which means they are more likely to stick with it. The payoff is having more energy to keep up with their active grandchildren, as well as the stamina to enjoy their travels.

"Some people have a hard time with retirement, but we're finding it very enjoyable," Dorothy enthused. "If you plan well and take care of your health, you can do some of the things you've always wanted to do. Spending time with our family, socializing with friends, and traveling around the world is keeping us happily busy. It's really a special time."

# CHAPTER FOUR

# Making Some Renovations: Your 70s

*"The wiser mind mourns less for what age takes away than what it leaves behind."*
—WILLIAM WORDSWORTH

### Never Stop Growing

*At 94, Sister Margaret was still quite active and mentally sharp. She worked in the communal kitchen every day and refused to give up kneeling at Mass, even though her knees were creaky and often complained loudly. When a longevity researcher asked her to what she attributed her vitality, she answered proudly, "I have an exercise program. I walk several miles each day." Amazed and curious, the researcher queried when she began her walking habit. "Oh, a long time ago," she replied. "I started walking when I was 70."*

Indeed, 24 years is a long time to be walking! However, the young man interviewing Sister Margaret was more impressed by the fact that she adopted this habit at the age of 70; a time when many can become "set in their ways." There is no doubt that daily exercise has contributed to the nun's health, but her mindset is an equally important ingredient to her longevity. Studies provide ample evidence that our willingness to remain open, to try new things, to adapt to changes, and continue to grow helps us age well.

It's true that aging and its effects can cause us to give up or modify some activities, but how we deal with those changes is a matter of attitude. If arthritis forces you to put away your tennis racket, you have two choices: stop playing tennis and do nothing, or replace tennis with a less strenuous but equally enjoyable activity. Often we reach a certain age and decide we are too old to try something new; to learn a new skill or adopt a new hobby. On the contrary, this is the perfect time to explore fresh interests. (See chapter 3 "Life Reimagined" to take an online assessment.)

## To Work or Not to Work

Retiring at the traditional age of 65 is increasingly becoming a thing of the past. Unfortunately, a large contributor to this trend is economic necessity. A recent survey by insurer Northwestern Mutual found that approximately 40 percent of Americans feel they can't afford to retire until their 70s or 80s. More specifically, 32 percent of those surveyed expect to work into their 70s, while 1 in 10 plan to be on the job into their 80s. On average, respondents plan on remaining in the workforce until the age of 68. Another 2013 survey conducted by Transamerica Center for Retirement Studies supported these results: 40 percent of these respondents stated that the economic recession has forced them to rethink retirement and work longer than planned. Over half (54 percent) said they will continue to work, at least part-time, after they "officially" retire.

Financial experts say that working into your 70s is a smart retirement move, as extending your career can help you grow your nest egg and ensure that you don't outlive your savings. After all, if you think about reaching the age of 95, then retiring at 65 means you will be living off of your savings for 30 years! As mentioned earlier, because a large number of jobs are now less labor intensive, involving computer and people skills instead of physical strength, it's possible to continue working well into one's senior years. So, if you are physically able, still find satisfaction in your job, and have employment opportunities, continuing to work is a good way to shore up your retirement funds.

Of course, not everyone's decision to prolong their career is based on economic necessity. According to the AARP, the majority of workers over the age of 70 report "really enjoying going to work." Of those folks still working after the age of 70, 30 percent hold professional or managerial positions, while 27 percent have clerical or sales jobs, and most of these positions are part-time. Some move from full-time positions to consulting roles, putting a lifetime of experience to good use. Another large group of "retirees" takes a complete departure from their previous career to pursue a long-time interest or do something they find meaningful, including volunteering within their community.

Continued education is also on the rise for older Americans. More than ever, we are seeing seniors going back to college to finish a degree or complete a graduate program—something they may have always dreamed of doing, but never got around to due to career and family obligations. While some might scoff at going back to school this late in life, studies show that continuing education not only opens the door to new career possibilities, it also keeps the mental juices flowing, improving cognitive health!

Whether you are working for a paycheck, pursuing a passion, embarking on a new career, or volunteering in the community, staying in the workforce can help you live longer. The key is doing something that provides meaning and fulfillment, as well as keeping you mentally engaged and socially connected.

## The Case for Older Workers

Though more seniors are choosing to extend their careers or take on a new job, staying in the workforce is not always easy. In fact, many employees are forced to retire before they anticipate. Older workers may have years of experience under their belts, but they often face age discrimination when seeking employment. In a 2009 report from the Sloan Center on Aging and Work, hiring managers listed a number of reasons for why they tend to reject older job applicants. They believed seniors were more likely to be burned out, resistant to new technologies, more likely to miss work due to illness, and have trouble working with younger supervisors. Similar studies show that many employers feel older workers are less creative and productive, and more expensive to employ.

To help dispel these myths, Peter Cappelli, a management professor at the Wharton School of Business, did some research of his own, which resulted in a 2010 book *Managing the Older Worker* (coauthored with former AARP CEO Bill Novelli). Cappelli looked at the common stereotypes regarding older workers across many fields and found they simply don't hold true.

In fact, older workers tend to be more loyal and reliable than their younger coworkers. They also have a larger network of contacts. Leadership skills, attention to detail, organization, listening skills, writing skills, and problem solving are all areas in which older workers received high marks from their employers. Capelli's findings also indicated that seniors in the workforce tend to be motivated by causes such as community, mission, and a chance to make the world a better place, while younger workers are more focused on salary and titles.

Of course, the greatest asset seniors bring to the workplace is experience. After years of gaining industry knowledge, learning how to work effectively with people, building relationships, and managing a wide variety of situations, older workers are usually capable of performing their jobs quicker, with fewer mistakes, while handling unexpected problems with ease. They often exhibit more patience and confidence when dealing with a crisis and can be instrumental in teaching younger coworkers to do the same.

All evidence suggests that if employers can look past a person's age and focus solely on abilities, they can benefit tremendously from hiring older workers. For seniors who are looking for employment, there are several things you can do to increase your chances. First, be sure to keep your computer skills up to date. If you need a refresher, sign up for a continuing education or online course. You can also take advantage of social media sites such as LinkedIn that focus on professional skills. It's a good idea to stay in touch with past coworkers and other professional contacts, because you never know from where an opportunity may come. And finally, experts recommend joining a professional group and attending the functions hosted by those groups. It may take more time and persistence, but as many older workers have discovered, finding the right job can help you age well.

## Evolving Happiness

*For many years, Elaine was part of a knitting club. A lifelong knitter, she enjoyed the creative process and working with her hands, but she also valued the company of the women who shared her passion. Unfortunately, as Elaine reached her late 70s, severe arthritis made it impossible for her to continue the hobby she loved. She reluctantly decided to quit the club. But, her friends wouldn't let her go. They urged her to continue coming to their weekly sessions, even though she could no longer knit.*

*"I was hesitant at first and a bit depressed," admitted Elaine. "I thought it might feel strange to just sit and talk while the other gals were busy knitting, but I came to realize the social aspect was just as important to me as the hobby."*

*Over time, several other members of the club were forced to put aside their knitting needles, but the group continued to meet, eventually becoming more of a book club. Through the years, these ladies have supported each other through good times (the birth of grandchildren) and bad (illnesses and the loss of spouses). They have filled the roles of cheerleaders, grief counselors, and health advisors for one another—and they are still going strong!*

This group illustrates the importance of maintaining strong, supportive social connections—something we've reiterated throughout these pages. It also demonstrates the benefits of being flexible and willing to evolve. With aging comes change, but it's how we cope with these changes that affects our well-being.

## Staying Active, Staying Social

We know that staying physically active and maintaining social connections are both important ingredients to aging well. So, why not combine the two and double the benefits?

- **Check out your local community center**—Many community centers offer special programs for seniors, including specifically designed exercise classes. Classes such as water aerobics, yoga, Tai Chi, and others not only provide a healthy dose of exercise, they're a good way to meet other like-minded seniors.
- **Walk with a friend**—Setting a regular time to walk with a friend or group of friends gives you time to socialize and stay connected—and makes it more difficult to skip!
- **Make your dates more active**—Having dinner with friends is great, but why not add a little variety to your social life with activities such as bowling, dancing, golf, bike riding, or walking in the park? Take turns planning activities and put regular dates on the calendar.

## Money Matters

The large percentage of people who expect to work into their 70s and even 80s due to economic concerns underscores the importance of sound financial planning. Even if you haven't been able to stash away a comfortable retirement account by now, there are ways to maximize your income, rebalance your investments, and manage your spending and savings more wisely to prepare for retirement. Unfortunately, research shows that many people are confused and afraid of the financial decisions that come with retiring. If you haven't already done so, experts recommend talking to a financial advisor who can help you plot a course for your retirement and outline some "catch-up" strategies.

"Planning your retirement can be like putting a puzzle together," says Michael Johnson, Certified Financial Planner (CFP)®, CPWA®. "A professional can help you put all the pieces together, including when to start taking Social Security benefits (you'll receive more if you wait) and pension plan distributions, as well as the tax implications of these decisions. There are also many investment options that can maximize your savings and provide future income streams."

You can find a local advisor through the Financial Planning Association (FPAnet.org), the National Association of Personal Financial Advisors (NAPFA.org), or CFP.net, which lists those who have received professional certification.

If you've already been working with a financial planner, now is the time to review and rebalance your assets, which should be done annually. "Your retirement plan should be re-evaluated as your life evolves. Having the right balance of money invested in stocks, bonds, and savings accounts relative to your overall retirement plan and risk tolerance can help protect you in an economic downfall," advises Johnson. "And let's face it, at this age you don't have time to make up significant losses."

At 70½, you are also required to start taking minimum distributions from IRA and 401(k) accounts; the amounts are based on account balances at the end of the previous year. As you get nearer to full retirement, financial experts also recommend the following:

- **Start reducing debt**—According to the Census Bureau, the average debt for Americans 65 and older more than doubled between 2000 and 2011. The biggest culprit is credit cards. It's important to reduce or eliminate as much high-interest debt as possible before retirement. Begin by paying off the highest-interest-rate debt first, while making minimum payments on the remainder. Once the highest-interest debt is paid down, move onto the next highest.
- **Consider refinancing or reverse mortgage**—If possible, your goal is to be mortgage free at retirement. However, if that's not feasible, you can consider other available options, such as taking out a home equity loan to help pay for living expenses. A reverse mortgage could also provide additional income, either through a lump sum payout or monthly checks. Keep in mind, reverse mortgages can be complex and involve many fees, so it's best to seek professional advice. Depending on your individual circumstances, refinancing your home may be a better choice.
- **Downsize your expenses**—For most people, moving to a smaller, less expensive home offers the biggest financial boost to their retirement. In addition to reducing or

eliminating mortgage payments, consider reducing taxes: Moving to an area with lower taxes can make a big difference in annual expenses—and it doesn't always mean moving far away. In some cases, a neighboring community can offer much lower taxes. Another way to reduce expenses is to sell your car (or one of two family vehicles), which eliminates a payment as well as insurance and maintenance fees. Many retirement communities offer transportation services, eliminating the need for a personal vehicle.

- **Create a pension**—If you won't be receiving a pension from your employer, you can convert a portion (20–25 percent) of your assets into an annuity, which provides a fixed lifetime income. In your 70s, your return on an annuity is higher than previous years because the older you are, the shorter your life expectancy and the higher your payout. If you are in good health and expecting to live many years, you may also consider longevity insurance, which is a type of deferred annuity that begins paying out at an advanced age (typically 85). However, if you pass away before that age, the money is lost.

- **Take control of your spending habits**—After retirement, a phenomenon called "spending creep" often occurs; folks spend more money than they planned in the first few years after retirement because they have more free time. They may find themselves going out to lunch or dinner more often, playing extra rounds of golf, or indulging the grandkids. Little splurges begin to add up and, before you know it, your savings are depleted. Although no one is fond of the idea, calculating and maintaining a budget are the best ways to prevent this type of spending. In some cases, grown children may be another drain on your retirement savings. According to an AARP survey, 23 percent of those in their 70s continue to offer financial support to their adult children. If this is a problem, experts suggest working together with a financial advisor, who can make discussing money issues more comfortable for both parents and grown children.

- **Reassess your insurance needs**—A financial expert can help you decide if the life insurance policy you bought when your children were born is still necessary. A better investment at this stage in life might be long-term care insurance or a longevity policy.

### Legal Issues

Does it surprise you to learn that an estimated 50 to 75 percent of the population never writes a will? Those who die intestate, which is a legal term meaning "without a will," often put their loved ones through unnecessary legal and financial hassles. Look at it this way: *you* can decide how you want your estate handled or let the probate court system make those decisions for you! A majority of people also never get around to spelling out their end-of-life wishes, which again causes undue stress on loved ones and leaves their care to chance. As we've discussed, legal experts recommend having at least three important documents in place:

- **A will** that outlines how property/assets will be dispersed, appoints legal guardians to minors or other dependents, and other personal requests
- **A living will** (including advance directives) that covers

healthcare decisions if you should become incapacitated and appoints a medical power of attorney

- **A durable power of attorney** that appoints someone to handle your financial affairs if you are unable to do so.

A fourth document to consider is a living trust, which appoints trustees to manage your property and other assets. You are the original trustee and therefore maintain control of your property; however, because a living trust "gathers" all property under one document, it allows for efficient distribution when you die, avoiding probate court.

Just as investments need regular reviews, legal documents should also be reassessed every year or so, and revised if necessary. Major life events such as marriage, birth of children/grandchildren, death of a spouse or other family member, a health crisis, or changes in tax laws may affect your decisions.

Again, these legal documents should be kept in a safe place in your home (e.g., a fireproof container or safe) along with insurance policies, account numbers, and information. It's also a good idea to have copies kept at an attorney's office. Loved ones should have copies of these documents and understand what they entail. They should also know where the originals are kept and how to access them if something should happen to you.

## Health Factors
### Staying Strong
*Henry knew he needed to get some exercise, particularly to maintain his strength. He was starting to notice it was becoming more difficult to get up and down from chairs, and in and out of the car—simple, everyday tasks. But the thought of joining a gym was unappealing. He had visions of young body-building types wearing muscle tees and over-eager fitness experts. Then,*

*one day, a friend mentioned the local community center, which offered a variety of senior programs, including exercise facilities. His friend recommended using the senior workout room. Of course, then Henry had an entirely different (but still unappealing) vision!*

*Grudgingly, he decided to check it out. To his surprise, Henry found a clean, no-frills workout facility, helpful attendants who understood the needs of older folks, and other active seniors. A physical therapist on staff helped him design a 40-minute workout that included strength-building exercises (machines set on lighter weights), along with 20 minutes on the recumbent bike, which he found much easier on his back and knees than a traditional exercise bike. Besides gaining strength and stamina, Henry reaped some unexpected benefits: he met several new friends and joined a poker club! He found he actually looked forward to his time at the "gym," and working out with his new buddies helped him stay motivated.*

Henry's experience is becoming more and more common

these days. As the population ages and communities recognize the importance of providing services geared toward seniors, we are seeing a growing number of senior centers and community complexes with senior amenities, including exercise facilities. In fact, some might say these centers are becoming the new coffee shop! It's a healthier setting in which to gather, stay active, learn something new, and catch up with friends. Contributing to this trend is a new focus on preventative care as many healthcare plans, including some Medicare Advantage plans, are now covering the cost of gym memberships for seniors and even offering free fitness/nutrition classes.

That's a step in the right direction, because as we've discussed, we lose muscle mass and bone density as we age, which means we must continually use our muscles to maintain strength. Core strength (abdominal muscles) in particular affect our ability to sit and stand, get up from the floor, enter and exit the car, keep our balance, and prevent back pain. In other words, when our core becomes weak from inactivity, we lose our ability to do the things we often take for granted, as well as prevent accidents.

### Avoiding the Vicious Cycle

By staying active, Henry was also able to avoid a phenomenon that physical therapists see all too often—the vicious cycle of sedentariness. After years of inactivity, muscles become weak, which leads to an injury, such as a fall. Once injured, the patient becomes fearful of falling again, so he/she scales back their activity level even further. The muscles become weaker and more inflexible, which leads to a higher risk of future injuries. And the cycle continues. It's not uncommon for rehabilitation centers to see the same patients over and over again.

Even if you've experienced an injury or have undergone surgery to replace a joint or repair a broken hip, exercise is necessary to heal, strengthen, and prevent problems going forward. If you are unsure of what type of exercise is right for you or what can be done within your personal limitations, it's best to consult a physical therapist. In addition, you should always talk to your physician before beginning an exercise program, particularly if you have been sedentary.

In general, seniors need to do a variety of exercises that cover four main areas:

- **Endurance**—Aerobic activities such as brisk walking, swimming, biking, or dancing are necessary to keep the heart strong and healthy. Any activity that increases your breathing and heart rate, performed for 30 minutes each day, will work. To ensure you are exercising at the right intensity, you can wear a heart monitor that displays your heart rate or track it manually. First determine your maximum heart rate, which is 220 minus your age. So, if you are 75, your maximum heart rate is approximately 145 beats per minute ($220 - 75 = 145$). Next, determine your target zone. Experts recommend exercising at 50 to 70 percent of your target heart rate for at least 30 minutes, which constitutes a moderate intensity workout. Therefore, the target zone for someone who is 75 is between 72.5 and 101.5 beats per minute.

- **Strength**—Exercises that increase muscle mass, strengthen muscles, and increase bone density may include lifting weights, using resistance bands or weight machines, or resisting your own body weight while performing crunches, bicep curls, leg lifts, etc. Strength-building exercises should be performed three days a week.

- **Balance**—Activities such as Tai Chi and yoga can improve strength and balance, but you can also perform a series of simple balance exercises at home. For example, while using a sturdy chair or wall for support, practice raising your toes and heels, lifting and holding one leg up at a time, and performing squats with your back against a wall. Balance exercises should be done several times a week.
- **Flexibility**—Activities such as yoga and Pilates, as well as regular stretching exercises, can keep your muscles flexible and your body limber, which helps prevent injury and back pain. Stretching can be done every day, particularly before and after other activities.

If you are unsure where to start, try visiting the National Institute on Aging website for a step-by-step guide to some sample exercises. Select drop-down menus Health and Aging, Publications, Topics Exercise at www.nia.nih.gov.

### Eating for Life

It goes without saying that maintaining a heart-healthy diet is important at any age (see chapter 2 for guidelines). However, when it comes to eating right, there are some special considerations as we get older. Many life changes and health issues can affect the way we eat, as well as what we eat. For instance, empty nesters often get out of the routine of cooking regular meals and find themselves snacking instead, which can be nutritionally deficient. It's important to eat three balanced meals, with healthy snacks in between, and to drink at least eight 8-ounce glasses of water each day.

Eating well often becomes more difficult for those living alone, who may ask "Why cook for one?" But, good nutrition is

vital as we age, and preparing fresh, healthy meals is the best way to eat nutritionally. Relying on packaged foods or take-out meals will increase your intake of sodium and saturated fats, while decreasing fiber and essential nutrients. If you're living alone and finding it difficult to prepare individual meals, try making larger servings, and then dividing and freezing portions for the future. You might also try getting together with friends for a cooking night, during which you make several dishes, divvy them up into freezer containers, and take home a variety of food. This is a great way to sample new recipes and socialize with friends.

"As we fight the effects of aging, which can take a toll on our bodies, we need to pack even more of a nutritional punch into our daily meals," says Susan Weiner, Registered Dietitian/ Nutritionist. "Many medical issues associated with aging, as well as the medications taken for those conditions, can actually deplete the body of important nutrients and cause problems with normal bodily functions. For instance, a number of medications cause digestive issues, including constipation. To combat these side effects, you can increase the amount of fiber you eat in your daily diet, while limiting the amount of processed and fatty foods that are known to exacerbate digestive problems. Think of food as your secret weapon!"

Weiner recommends the following tips for healthy eating in our senior years:

- **Fuel your body with a variety of healthy foods** throughout the day. By eating meals and snacks that are well-spaced, you will increase your energy level and keep blood sugar on an even keel. Of course, it's important to keep calories in mind. The number of calories you consume will depend on your age, gender, body size, and activity level. General guidelines for women over 50 recommend consuming between 1,600 and 2,200 calories per day depending on activity level, while men over 50 should take in between 2,000 and 2,400 calories per day depending on activity level. If you are trying to lose weight, the number of calories should be reduced.
- **Cut back on fruit juices,** which may add a lot of sugar and calories to your diet, without the benefits of fiber. Choose fresh fruits and vegetables instead, and drink water for hydration. Sugary soft drinks should also be avoided.
- **Eat a wide assortment of foods.** Not only will eating the same foods every day eventually lead to boredom, it won't provide a complete spectrum of nutrients. Choose from a

variety of lean proteins (chicken, fish, turkey, lean pork and beef), whole grains, fruits and vegetables, and low-fat dairy products—and be creative! Foods that are richest in vitamins and minerals are typically more vibrant, so a colorful plate is a healthy plate (e.g., green—broccoli, spinach, kale, and asparagus; orange—carrots and sweet potatoes; red—beets, apples, and berries; yellow—squash, peppers, pears, and bananas; purple—eggplant and cabbage).

- **Drink plenty of water.** As we get older, we are less naturally thirsty, but more prone to dehydration. By the time you feel thirsty, you're already getting dehydrated. If you don't feel thirsty throughout the day, set up regular reminders to drink water and keep a glass or other container of water with you as you go about your daily activities. However, try to limit your water intake after dinner to prevent waking up during the night to urinate and interrupting your sleep.

- **Choose whole grain foods** (i.e., brown rice vs. white rice, whole wheat bread vs. refined white flour). Read the nutritional labels on breads and cereals to make sure they have at least 5 grams of fiber per serving (more is better). Whole grains (fiber) not only help reduce cholesterol and improve cardiovascular health, they improve digestive function.

Weiner also suggests asking your physician to test your vitamin $B_{12}$ and vitamin D levels during your annual exam, as well as testing for anemia. Vitamin deficiencies, particularly $B_{12}$ and D, become more common as we get older. In addition to making dietary changes, your physician may recommend a supplement(s) to get you back on track nutritionally.

## Healthy Snack Ideas

Snacking can be good for you. In fact, according to Susan Weiner, Registered Dietitian/Nutritionist and Diabetes Educator, eating throughout the day (three balanced meals with snacks in between) is a good way to keep your energy up and get a variety of nutrients. The trick, of course, is making those snacks healthy, and keeping total calorie intake in a range that's right for you. Good snack choices include:

- **High-fiber vegetables**—It can sometimes be difficult to squeeze the recommended 5 to 8 servings of vegetables a day into three meals, so snacking on them is a great way to meet your daily requirements. To make veggies more enticing, try dipping carrots, red pepper, or celery in some hummus or mashed avocado, which gives you the added benefit of protein. If chewing raw vegetables is an issue, steam your veggies first or make a batch of vegetable soup. Yes, soup is a great snack! Add sliced sweet potato and some beans to the soup for a delicious and nutritious snack.

- **Fruit**—For the best taste and lowest cost, choose whatever fruit is in season, or buy frozen fruit (without added sugar). For variety and a little protein boost, spread your apple or banana slices with 1 to 2 tablespoons of peanut butter (preferably natural peanut butter, which has less sodium and sugar). If fruit is difficult to chew, try a baked apple, sprinkled with cinnamon or all-natural applesauce. Fresh or frozen fruit combined with low-fat yogurt or milk and blended makes a tasty and nutritious smoothie.

- **Low-fat dairy products**—Low-fat yogurt and cottage cheese are good snack choices. You can top it off with fresh fruit such as blueberries or strawberries for some natural sweetness. If you can tolerate nuts, try sprinkling your yogurt with some slivered almonds or crushed walnuts. A few small slices of cheese on whole grain crackers is another tasty option.

- **Nuts or nut butters**—A handful of almonds, pistachios, or walnuts can be a high-protein, heart-smart snack. Keep in mind, however, that nuts are high in fat and calories, so portion size is important. Try spreading one to two tablespoons of natural peanut butter or natural almond butter on a few whole grain crackers or a slice of whole grain bread.

- **A hard-boiled egg** is also a good high-protein grab-and-go snack. Far too often, when we think of snacks, we think of convenient packaged goods such as salty chips and pretzels or sugary baked goods. But these foods are typically empty calories that provide no nutritional value to our diet and, in fact, can sabotage our health. By training ourselves to reach for healthy, nutritious snacks we can fuel our bodies and ward off chronic conditions such as high blood pressure, high cholesterol, and type 2 diabetes.

- **Far too often, when we think of snacks,** we think of convenient packaged goods such as salty chips and pretzels or sugary baked goods. But these foods are typically empty calories that provide no nutritional value to our diet and, in fact, can sabotage our health. By training ourselves to reach for healthy, nutritious snacks we can fuel our bodies and ward off chronic conditions such as high blood pressure, high cholesterol, and diabetes.

### Timing Is Everything

*Kevin limped into the house, swallowed a couple of ibuprofen, and grabbed the ice pack from the freezer. With a groan, he sat on the couch and propped up his knee, which was painful and swollen—again. He had already given up his daily walk, and now even a leisurely round of golf was enough to aggravate his knee. His doctor had told Kevin several years ago that he may need a knee replacement, but who had time for that? Sure, thought Kevin, they could do some amazing things these days with joint replacements, but there was still a recovery period and physical therapy to contend with, so he kept putting it off. Now, the pain was nearly constant, and he found himself severely limiting his activities, which only made the situation worse.*

*At his wife's urging, Kevin finally went back to his orthopedist, who warned that postponing his surgery would only make the recovery more difficult and the results less effective. With a sigh, he agreed to put a date on the calendar. It was time to reclaim his once active life.*

*After his knee replacement surgery, Kevin spent five days in the hospital. He was surprised that the nurses had him up and walking the day after surgery, and starting rehabilitation before he was even released. Three months later, with diligent physical therapy, Kevin was back on the golf course and pleased to find that he was pain free. It made him wonder why he waited so long.*

Let's face it, surgery is no fun—even with today's advanced medical procedures—so we tend to wait. But with many surgeries, timing is critical; postponing necessary procedures can lead to complications and affect future mobility. For instance, several studies have proven that knee replacement surgery performed *before* severe stiffness and pain set in is associated with better outcomes. In some cases, if a patient waits too long, insurance will no longer cover certain procedures due to age and risk. On the other hand, conditions that are caught early may allow you to take advantage of less invasive procedures such as arthroscopic surgeries, which involve smaller incisions and less recovery time. Of course, it works the other way, too. Most joint replacements will last 15 to 20 years, so if surgery is performed on someone young, they may need another replacement down the road.

If you have knee pain and are considering surgery, you're not alone. Today, more than 600,000 knee replacement surgeries (also known as knee arthroplasty) are performed annually in the United States The majority of these patients are 65 and older, and the most common reason for this type of surgery is age-related osteoarthritis, which is caused by normal wear and tear of the knee joint. It's estimated that 27 million Americans suffer from osteoarthritis, which causes inflammation and the gradual breakdown and eventual loss of cartilage in the joints. Because cartilage cushions the ends of the bones and allows easy joint movements, the breakdown of cartilage causes bones to rub together leading to stiffness, pain, and loss of movement. While hard-working knees are most often affected, hips, lower back, neck, and finger joints can all develop osteoarthritis. It's a common affliction, but it doesn't always lead to surgery.

### Improving Mobility without Surgery
When treated early, osteoarthritis, like many other issues that affect mobility, can often be treated with a combination of medication and physical therapy. Nonsteroidal anti-inflammatory drugs are used to reduce inflammation and pain, while physical therapy improves strength and movement, which is essential.

"When we start experiencing pain in a joint, it's natural to want to limit our activity and avoid the discomfort," says Wendy Conlon, Licensed Physical Therapist (MSPT). "But, stopping all movement is the worst thing you can do. Moving your joints keeps them flexible and reduces stiffness. It's a matter of choosing activities that are easy on the joints, such as walking or swimming. In addition, targeted exercises can strengthen the muscles that support the joint, reducing pain and increasing ease of movement."

Another way to improve joint health and possibly avoid surgery involves your body weight. According to research published in 2013 in the *Journal of the American Medical Associa-*

*tion (JAMA)*, if you are overweight, losing 10 percent of your body weight can significantly reduce pain and improve mobility in those suffering from osteoarthritis of the knee. In fact, the study showed that the more weight loss, the greater the improvements, due to decreased joint load and reduced inflammation. That's because obesity is a major risk factor for knee osteoarthritis, and excess body weight often exacerbates the pain and disability associated with the condition.

Whether its medication and physical therapy, weight loss, or a minimally invasive procedure, it's important to consider all the alternatives before electing surgery. It's also wise to obtain a second medical opinion. All surgery involves risks and potential complications, and though 90 percent of patients who undergo joint replacements return to normal function, 10 percent report some level of continued pain and/or limited mobility after surgery. When deciding on a procedure, physicians consider the severity of the pain and the degree of disability, as well as a patient's general health. The bottom line: With so many treatment options available today, there's no reason to bench yourself or live with unnecessary pain. Be sure to talk to your physician about any joint pain you may be experiencing early on, when treatment can be the most effective.

### Can We Talk about Incontinence?

It's a common issue—in fact an estimated 13 million people in the United States (85 percent of whom are women) suffer from it—but incontinence can be difficult to talk about. Urinary incontinence, which involves the involuntary leakage of urine, becomes more prevalent as people age according to Dr. Benjamin Brucker, an Assistant Professor of Urology at NYU Langone Medical Center with expertise in incontinence.

"However, urinary incontinence is not a part of aging that you have to just live with," says Brucker.

A system of ligaments, muscles, and nerves around the bladder and urethra works together to prevent urine leakage; when something interferes with these signals or the support becomes weak, incontinence can be the result. More specifically, incontinence can occur if:

- **The bladder** squeezes at the wrong time or contracts too hard.
- **The support ligaments** and/or muscles around the urethra (called the urinary sphincter) are weak or damaged.
- **The bladder** doesn't empty completely as it should.
- **Something blocks the urethra,** such as an enlarged prostate.

There are a few different types of urinary incontinence symptoms, but when thinking about causes and treatments for incontinence, the two most common complaints are stress incontinence and urgency incontinence (with overactive bladder). Stress incontinence is when urine leaks while laughing or coughing, for instance; while urgency incontinence is when leakage of urine is associated with urgency, usually caused by muscle spasms. In women, multiple pregnancies, being overweight, and even menopause can increase the risk of developing incontinence. In men, prostate issues (including prior prostate surgery) and obesity can lead to urinary issues. There are also some genetic factors and underlying health conditions, such as diabetes or neurologic problems, that may cause urinary incontinence. In general, incontinence can often be avoided by:

- limiting caffeine and alcohol (known bladder irritants)
- keeping weight in a healthy range
- not smoking

- avoiding chronic constipation by eating a healthy, high-fiber diet
- doing pelvic floor (Kegel) exercises to strengthen the muscles that support the bladder and urethra.

If you are dealing with incontinence, the first step is to talk with your physician and determine the type and cause. "Often just talking with an expert will help a patient realize that something as simple as avoiding a cup of tea before bed can have a tremendous positive impact," notes Brucker. "I often start by having patients keep a log for a day or two of the fluids they drink, how often they urinate, and what is going on when they have an accident."

There are a number of medications available to treat an overactive bladder, as well as products that offer discreet protection. If muscle weakness is the problem, doing pelvic floor exercises, often called Kegel exercises, can prevent or significantly improve incontinence. Believe it or not, these exercises can also help with frequent urination and urgency incontinence caused by bladder spasms. Here's what to do:

- **Squeeze** the same muscles you would use to stop the flow of urine. These are internal muscles, so your belly and buttocks should not move when you do this.
- **Hold** for three seconds and then relax for three seconds.
- **Repeat** 10–15 times per session and do two to three sessions each day.

It requires frequent repetition to successfully strengthen pelvic floor muscles, but the exercises can be done inconspicuously, while driving, reading, watching television, or other random times throughout the day. Dr. Brucker does warn his patients that overdoing it can lead to the muscles being fatigued when you need them, such as during a coughing spell. The key is to do these exercises regularly, but not constantly throughout the day. While strengthening the pelvic floor can be very effective, physical therapists caution that the key is starting early. The longer the problem goes on and the weaker the muscles become, the more difficult it will be to strengthen them and eventually it will be impossible to correct the problem.

## Making Your Home Safe

*It was stupid, really. At least that's what Donna thought in hindsight. She had gotten her foot caught on the edge of that rug more times than she could count, but there it was, still next to the bed, where it had been for years. Then one morning, while in a rush, Donna stumbled on the rug and fell hard, banging her knee on the bedpost and landing with a sickening thud on her hip. But Donna was lucky; though her hip and knee were both badly bruised, nothing was broken—this time. The accident left her limping for a week and thinking about changes.*

*"That fall opened my eyes," confessed Donna. "At 72, I didn't think of myself as old enough to worry about things like falls and broken hips, but now I realize it can happen to anybody in an instant."*

Too often, we wait for a nasty fall or other injury before we make changes around the house. After all, no one likes to admit that they may be more susceptible to age-related accidents. We may joke about needing different eyeglasses for every occasion or the knee that gives out once in a while, but these impairments, though they may be minor, can make our homes unsafe. Isn't it better to take preventative measures than to deal with the consequences after an accident occurs?

Physical therapists recommend a number of safety measures to prevent accidents in and around your home, including:

## Outside

- Make sure entryways, including walkways, exterior steps, and porches, are in good repair, free of debris, and with no crumbling edges or broken boards.
- Install a secure railing that is easy to grasp with both hands.
- Use lights to illuminate a wide area of the yard and walkway from the parking area to the entrance.
- Smooth out or eliminate the doorway threshold, or make sure it's well marked.

## Inside—Living Areas

- Walkways should be wide enough to pass through using a walker or wheelchair, if necessary.
- Pathways should be free of clutter, with no electric or phone cords running across walkways or open areas.
- Be sure carpets and large rugs are tacked down securely, with no frayed or rolling edges, and eliminate throw rugs.
- Use adequate lighting with accessible switches that can be turned on without walking across a dark room.
- Sofas and chairs should be high and firm enough for easy sitting and rising.
- All stairways should be free of clutter and loose rugs and have secure handrails and proper lighting.

## Bathrooms

- Doorways should be wide enough to pass through when using a walker or wheelchair, if necessary.
- Floors should be free of clutter without throw rugs.
- Install strong, secure grab bars in shower/bath and near the toilet.
- Consider using a shower seat or walk-in tub.
- Make sure the floor of the tub and/or shower has a

non-skid surface.

- If the toilet seat is not high enough for easy use, consider using a raised toilet seat.

### Bedroom

- Make sure the floor is clutter free without loose rugs.
- The path between the bed and the bathroom should be free of clutter and well lit.
- Use adequate lighting with accessible switches that can be turned on without walking across a dark room.
- There should be an accessible phone near the bed.
- A chair with armrests and firm seating is recommended to avoid falls while dressing.

### Kitchen

- Floor space should be free of clutter and throw rugs.
- Floor should not be waxed or slippery.
- Make sure pathways are wide enough to accommodate a walker or wheelchair, if necessary.
- Make everyday kitchen items easily accessible at knee or waist height to avoid excessive bending and reaching.
- Chairs should be firm and stable, without casters or rollers.

Of course, general safety measures, such as smoke alarms on each floor, a carbon monoxide detector, and a working fire extinguisher, are musts for every home. It's also a good idea to have emergency and physician numbers in a location that is easily accessible or programmed into the phone.

Before a patient returns home from the hospital or rehabilitation facility after a fall or other injury, a physical therapist is often required to conduct a home safety assessment, which includes a checklist like the one featured above. Their job is to ensure that the patient has a safe living environment, thus avoiding another incident. But why wait until after an accident to make your home safer when you can take some simple steps now?

Of course, there may come a time when basic safety measures are not enough. For instance, if you are having trouble with stairs, a home with multiple floors may simply be too hazardous or unlivable. In some cases, it can be cost-prohibitive to retrofit older homes with wider passageways and user-friendly bath fixtures. Depending on the type of mobility issue with which you are dealing, it may be time to consider a move (see "A Retirement or Independent Living Community May Be Right for You").

## To Stay Healthy, 70-Somethings Should

- **Continue following** a heart-healthy diet and exercising regularly.
- **Reduce sodium** to less than 2,000 mg per day (less than 1,500 mg if possible, particularly if you have been diagnosed with hypertension).
- **Have annual physical exams** and schedule necessary health screenings.
- **Know your numbers**— have blood pressure checked annually. If you have been diagnosed with high blood pressure and are taking medication, home monitoring may be advised. Have cholesterol and blood glucose levels checked every two to five years, depending on your personal risk factors. If these numbers are elevated, tests should be performed more frequently.
- **Take all medications as directed**—never discontinue or change medication schedules without consulting your physician.
- **Discuss the necessity** and proper timing of surgeries, such as joint replacements with your physician.
- **Make your home safe** by removing tripping hazards, improving lighting, and installing safety rails and grab bars.

## A Retirement or Independent Living Community May Be Right for You

Living in a bustling college town was not what Mark and Leann envisioned for their retirement years. But, when they noticed a new senior housing complex opening near a major university, they decided to check it out. They had spent time around the campus while their oldest son was attending college and had enjoyed the shops, restaurants, cultural opportunities, and nearby parks. However, they had never thought of the urban setting as a place to retire. The idea was intriguing.

"We really liked the idea of being able to walk around town," Mark explained. "Of course, they also offer transportation services and other amenities that were starting to sound good."

Their two-story colonial had seemed small while raising two active boys. Sports equipment, backpacks, and a revolving door of friends had filled the rooms to overflowing. However, now that the kids were grown and starting their own families, the house felt too big. (It made Leann smile to hear her sons complain about their homes being cluttered with large plastic toys!)

"We love our house because it's filled with so many good memories," Leann said wistfully. "But it's starting to become more than we can handle. It used to take me a few hours to clean; now it takes me all day and my back aches from the effort."

Mark shared similar feelings: "I always loved working in the yard, but now a day of yard work means a day with the ice pack! The stairs are getting to me, too. If I forget something upstairs, I usually just leave it until later," he chuckled.

Still, they were ambivalent about moving to a retirement community. They wondered if they might be bored without household tasks. If they downsized, who would host Thanksgiving? Would the kids be upset if they sold the house? It was a big decision, so they decided to take a practical approach by comparing costs. First, they determined the price of hiring cleaning services, lawn care, and snow removal. When combined with monthly utility bills, taxes, and general maintenance, they found it was actually more cost-effective to live in the new retirement community.

"It makes financial sense," admitted Mark. "But, in the end, it was the appeal of having less responsibility and more time to enjoy our retirement that sold us on the move. And, the lively atmosphere was a nice surprise."

Many people are surprised by the diversity of retirement communities these days. The industry has grown dramatically and is forecasted to expand at an even faster pace over the next two decades. It's a trend being driven by more than 80 million baby boomers (as estimated by the U.S. Census Bureau), who are currently retiring or expected to retire within 6 to 10 years, and are interested in new living arrangements. That kind of demand has led to a wide array of options in specialized housing and services for seniors.

Whether they're called retirement villages, independent living, or senior housing, these communities come in many sizes and settings, from cozy studio apartments to clusters of independent homes and spacious townhouses. They are located in and around bustling urban settings, quiet suburban neighborhoods, and sunny golf courses. Some, like the one Mark and Leann found appealing, are associated with major universities and offer residents free classes. What these communities have in common are services and amenities geared toward seniors. Here, too, one can find a wide range of offerings.

In general, retirement or independent living communities provide housekeeping, home maintenance, daily meals, the opportunity for social activities, and transportation for errands, shopping, and appointments. Some communities offer expanded amenities such as fitness programs, garden centers, computer labs, and libraries. The idea of freeing yourself from daily chores and the worry of home maintenance may be the biggest draw for some, but others find the opportunity to socialize and develop friendships just as appealing.

When deciding on a retirement community, it's important to find the right fit. Experts suggest starting with a list of priorities—what's really important to you? If being close to family and friends is key, begin by narrowing your search geographically. Is it vital to live in a strong faith-based community, or one that offers easy access to outdoor activities or other interests? Do you prefer a quiet, laid-back environment, or one that's lively and filled with activities? Which services and amenities are most essential to you?

The next step is to begin researching options that meet your criteria. Websites such as retirenet.com and retirementliving.com allow you to search for options by location and lifestyle. It's also important to compare total costs, which can differ widely. While some communities require you to purchase a unit and then charge monthly fees for services, others are rental homes with services included in the monthly or annual payment. Finally, spend some time visiting the property, talking with the residents, sampling a meal, and getting a feel for the atmosphere. You may be pleasantly surprised to find interesting menus and livelier activities, as these communities attempt to attract a new generation of seniors.

*In the end, Mark and Leann made the move and were glad they did. Their new apartment was private, but allowed them to be part of a larger community. They made some new friends, but were close enough to the old neighborhood to maintain their long-standing friendships. Spending Saturday mornings at the local farm market instead of mowing the lawn or cleaning the house was a pleasant change. Initially, Leann was still concerned about hosting the holidays, which she had done for many years. But as it turned out, her daughter-in-law was happy to step in.*

*"I guess it's time for the next generation to take over," said Leann with a smile. "It's kind of nice to just show up with my famous pumpkin pie!"*

## Staying Vibrant
### *Brain Games*

Memory loss can rob us of vibrant senior years. It can be frustrating and downright scary to lose our mental acuity, but it's not inevitable. Throughout life, our brain can remodel itself, responding to a person's experiences. This ability is known as neuroplasticity, and in simple terms, it means that the brain, much like your bicep, can stay fit with exercise.

Exercise relates to the brain in two ways. First, physical exercise can benefit your brain by reducing stress hormones and increasing chemicals in the body that nourish brain cells. Second, exercising the brain itself can enhance mental function, improve memory, and ward off dementia. In other words, keeping the brain engaged and stimulated can help us maintain cognitive health. There are many ways to exercise the brain, including:

- **Learn something new**—Brush up on your computer skills, master another language, try a new craft, learn to play a musical instrument—the possibilities are endless.
- **Play brain games**—Any game that involves memory, concentration, speed, problem-solving, and attention will do the trick. To get started, grab your favorite crossword, sudoku, or word puzzle, go to www.luminosity.com, or download a number of available apps for your smartphone.
- **Join the grandkids**—The next time the grandchildren ask to play video or computer games, say "yes," as long as you get to play along!
- **Practice mindful awareness or meditation**—Some may think of meditation as "thinking of nothing," but in actuality practicing mindful awareness or meditation

involves focusing your attention on something specific—
a word, a phrase, a pleasant place, etc. It requires concentration to shut out distractions, rid your mind of
unwanted thoughts, and simply be aware of the present
moment. Numerous studies show that meditation not
only reduces levels of the stress hormone cortisol, which
can be damaging to the body, but can also improve
memory. Even more compelling are the results of a 2005
study that showed that people who meditated regularly
had thicker cortical walls than non-meditators, which
means their brains were aging at a slower rate. Cortical
thickness is also associated with decision making,
attention, and memory. Guided meditations, as well as
easy instructions and smartphone apps, are available on
many websites, including www.meditationoasis.com.

### Social Connections
At the risk of sounding like a broken record, socialization is
important to aging well and maintaining our vibrancy. In fact,

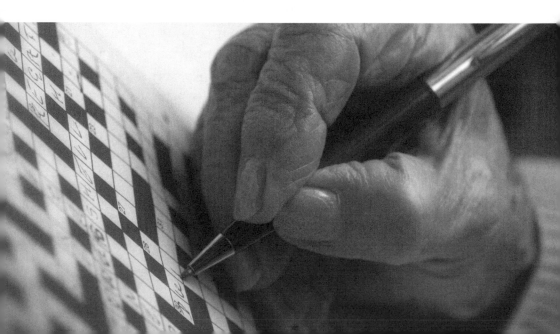

according to one study, neglecting our social networks can be as harmful to our health as smoking up to 15 cigarettes daily! For some, staying social comes naturally, while others have to make an effort. It can also become more challenging for seniors who have lost spouses and live alone or are residing far from other family members to stay connected with others.

As our life circumstances change, it's natural for relationships to evolve. When we graduate from high school or college and begin careers or start families, some friendships may fizzle out. Later, we might form temporary bonds with coworkers or the parents of our children's friends, which dissolve when we change jobs or our children become adults. As we get older and become less involved with careers and school activities, it can be difficult to expand our social circles. So, how can we build and maintain a strong network of friends later in life?

The first step is to get out of the house! Making acquaintances on social media sites is not the same as forming true friendships and interacting in person. Joining a club is one way to meet other like-minded seniors. With a little research, you'll find there are clubs for virtually every interest, from books and crafting, to poker and purple hats. You might also check out the local community center or senior center, which typically offers a variety of activities and outings. Volunteering at a local charity, church, or hospital provides an opportunity to not only meet other people, but engage in a meaningful activity. And, if you're lucky enough to have a good social network, be sure to make an effort to maintain those bonds—schedule regular dates with friends and family. Think of spending time with friends as a prescription for good health and insurance for the years ahead!

## Words of Wisdom . . .

After running his own restaurant and pizzeria for 35 years, George decided to sell the business and retire. After all, he had worked long hours, often six or seven days a week for many years, and felt it was time to take a break. His "retirement" lasted approximately four months!

"I was in my early 60s and used to being very active, always surrounded by customers and staff," recalled George. "Suddenly being at home alone, with my wife still working, was very difficult for me. It was also hard on my wife, who hinted that I needed to find something to keep me occupied. So, I took a part-time job as a prep cook, and 20 years later, I was still going to work."

It was during this subsequent career that George was forced to take a break. In 2004, he underwent cardiac bypass surgery, followed by months of rehabilitation, during which he learned the importance of eating well and exercising regularly. It was the threat of slowing down that prompted him to join a gym and make exercise a habit. He soon found a gym partner to encourage attendance and that duo eventually became a quartet. While some people may have quit working at this point, George's longing for social connections sent him back to the kitchen part-time.

George officially retired, for the second time, at the age of 84. The catalyst came when his wife fell and broke her leg, which required George to care for her full-time during recovery. Even while being a caretaker, however, George was back at the gym with "the guys."

"Now, I spend five days a week with my 'men's club,'" said George fondly. "We're really just a group of retired and semi-retired guys who get together at the gym every morning to work out and then have coffee. Even if I have a day when I don't feel like exercising, it's hard to skip because we go as a group. The exercise is good, but the chance to talk and share gossip is more important."

In addition to hitting the gym and catching up, George and his friends like to play cards—a pastime that occasionally turns into all-night poker tournaments. George also belongs to a close-knit faith family and attends a variety of church events. Next year, he and his wife have a sixth trip to Greece planned, which is George's homeland, and hope to visit their son in California.

"My grown son likes to joke that instead of me worrying about his whereabouts, he has to worry about what his 87-year-old dad is up to," George laughed. "He says my social calendar is busier than his. That may be true, because I think it's essential to belong to a 'community' as you get older—people who keep you motivated and give you a positive outlook. When you're active and spending time with people you love, doing things you enjoy, then age is just a number. I always say it's not how old you are, but how you feel, and I feel good."

# CHAPTER FIVE

# Adding On:
# Your 80s and Beyond

*"It's not how old you are; it's how you are old."*
—JULES RENARD

### Losing the Stigma

*Clare was often described as "spry" and "feisty," and she liked it that way. At 84, she was living independently, enjoying time with her family and friends, and had just adopted a stray cat who loved cuddling in her lap. So, when the doctor suggested she use a walker, Clare, who never took suggestions easily, balked. Though she had been using a cane to help steady herself for several years, she thought of walkers as something "for feeble old people," which she was not (well, at least she wasn't feeble). An observant man, the doctor had noticed her unsteady gait (her medications sometimes made her woozy) and the way she leaned heavily on her cane to get up from the chair (arthritis was making things difficult).*

*Still, Clare didn't see the need for a walker, which she thought of as bulky and cumbersome. The doctor pointed out that a walker would not only make things easier, it might possibly prevent a fall. Of course, her daughter had agreed with the doctor, reminding Clare that she had a stumble while they were leaving the grocery store recently (that darn uneven pavement!). Clare knew that once her daughter got something in her head, she would never hear the end of it, so she agreed to think about it.*

*The weeks went by, and despite her daughter's insistence, Clare would not agree to use a walker—until the accident occurred. On the way to the bathroom one night, she caught her foot on the doorway threshold, lost her balance, and fell. It happened so fast that Clare didn't have a chance to grab hold of anything. She landed with a sickening thud on the hard tile floor and instantly felt a sharp, intense pain in her hip. Grateful for the medical alert button she wore around her wrist, she called for help and waited anxiously for the ambulance to arrive.*

There is a stigma associated with things like canes, walkers, and wheelchairs. Just as Clare did, we tend to see them as signs of becoming old and helpless; the first step in the loss of mobility and independence. But, in many ways, these tools are the opposite—they help seniors maintain their mobility and independence, as well as prevent serious injuries.

"Instead of associating aids such as canes and walkers and home safety measures such as grab bars and railings with dependence, we should equate them with independence, because that's what they help us preserve," says Wendy Conlon, Licensed Physical Therapist (MSPT). "Being mobile is critical to living independently, so we shouldn't discount any tool that supports mobility and prevents disabling injuries."

*After weeks of rehabilitation, Clare was able to return home, with one condition—she must agree to use a walker. In hindsight, she realized the pain and recovery of a hip replacement may have been avoided if she had started using a walker when she first starting feeling unsteady, but the past was past. Going forward, she was determined to prevent another accident, if possible, and even more resolved to maintain her independence. She did, however, get the brightest red walker she could find. Clare was still feisty, after all.*

### Aging in Place

Like Clare, most seniors would prefer to remain independent for as long as possible and stay in their own home, whether that home is the same one they've lived in for most of their life or an apartment in a retirement community where they've resided comfortably for years. This desire to stay put is often referred to as "aging in place."

Fortunately, aging in place is easier to achieve today than it once was thanks to a growing number of products and services designed to help seniors live independently. For instance, medical procedures such as joint replacements are keeping seniors mobile longer. For those who need a little help, home aides are available to assist with a wide range of services, from personal care to meal preparation. To assist seniors in getting around, many communities and retirement villages offer free transportation. In addition, medical alert products and remote monitoring technology provide peace of mind for both seniors and their caregivers. And, of course, almost anything can be delivered right to your door!

## Consult an Aging-in-Place Specialist

A new sort of consultant, called Certified Aging-in-Place Specialist (CAPS), is helping seniors live safely and comfortably in their homes—with a touch of style. The CAPS program was developed by the National Association of Home Builders, in partnership with the AARP and the NAHB Research Center, to teach professionals how to modify homes for aging in place. This encompasses a wide range of projects, from installing user-friendly light switches for someone with arthritis to renovating an entire home for someone who is wheelchair bound.

More often than not, major renovations are not necessary to make a home livable, experts say. Most houses need a little fine tuning, which may include removing thresholds or adjusting doorway casings to accommodate walkers or wheelchairs, changing the layout of furniture, installing grab bars and railings, and perhaps replacing flooring—seniors with balance issues, or those who use a walker or wheelchair, find it easier to get around on hardwood floors instead of carpet.

An Aging-in-Place Specialist may also recommend replacing some furniture with pieces designed specifically for mobility issues, such as a lift chair that helps you get up and down with ease or a counter-height table that makes dining more comfortable. The good news is many of these products are now available in stylish fabrics and finishes, so your home doesn't have to resemble a hospital room. Lift chairs can be found in a choice of fabrics and designs, while new grab bars are designed to resemble towel bars in finishes such as brass, chrome, and bronze to match any décor. And for those who require larger projects such as stair lifts or walk-in tubs, a CAPS remodeler can recommend solutions that are both ergonomic and economical.

It all begins with a consultation to assess your individual needs, both current and future. A CAPS encourages seniors to make proactive changes, helping them to anticipate possible issues and thus avoid another renovation down the road. You can locate a Certified Aging-in-Place Specialist at www.nahb.org.

## Health Factors
### *Staying Functionally Active*
Aging in place requires seniors to remain functionally active, which simply means being able to perform daily living tasks, such as getting around the house without assistance, using the toilet, showering and dressing, and making meals. As we've discussed, the best way to remain functionally active is to stay active throughout the aging process. Exercises that build strength and preserve balance go a long way toward maintaining independence. (See chapter 4 for exercise tips.)

Unfortunately, many people stop exercising after an injury or surgery, or when a condition such as arthritis or stenosis makes movement difficult. However, it doesn't matter if you are walking without assistance, using a walker, or confined to a wheelchair; whether you have severe arthritis or spinal issues; there is some form of exercise that can be done to improve functionality. Movement, no matter how small, is better than no movement.

In fact, a lack of motion can often lead to frozen joint syndrome, technically known as adhesive capsulitis. This painful disorder results from chronic inflammation, scarring, thickening, and shrinkage of the capsule that surrounds the joint, which "freezes" the joint in place. While shoulders and knees are most commonly affected, it can occur in other joints. Frozen joints typically develop after a surgery or injury, following prolonged immobilization or extremely reduced motion of a joint.

Fortunately, immobile joints can be "unfrozen" with a combination of pain management and physical therapy, which gradually restores the range of motion by loosening the fibrous bands of tissue or adhesions that have been allowed to develop between the joint surfaces. The process is often slow. In some cases, where movement has not occurred for a very long time, it becomes necessary for an orthopedic surgeon to break the adhesions. To avoid this type of surgery, which may lead to further complications, it's important to keep moving.

Joint pain, to varying degrees, is a common malady as we get older. As with many other issues related to aging, exercise can reduce discomfort and ward off more serious problems. Working with a physical therapist can help you find the right exercises for your individual situation; however, the following generally recommended exercises that keep joints flexible, improve range of motion, and maintain strength are a good place to start:

### Range of Motion

- **Arm Circles** help improve range of motion in the shoulder joints. Start by placing your arms straight out to your side and begin moving them in small circles. Gradually increase the size of the circle until you reach your range limit. Once there, repeat a few times and then change the direction of your circles and gradually make them smaller. Range of motion exercises such as arm circles should be performed at least every other day.
- **Leg Lifts**—To keep hip joints flexible, we need to perform hip abduction exercises such as leg lifts. Lie on your right side with your right knee bent. Slowly lift your left leg until it is about two feet in the air. Lower it slowly and repeat. When finished with your set, change sides and repeat with the other leg. (Note: If you have had a hip replacement, consult your physician or physical therapist before starting an exercise routine.)

### Strengthening

- **Squats**—Strengthening exercises such as squats will help build strong muscles that protect and support your joints. To perform a squat, stand with your feet even with your hips and your toes facing straight ahead. Bend your knees and lower your hips (do not let your knees extend over your toes), keeping your body straight and stomach pulled in tightly. Hold for a few seconds and straighten up. Repeat the process as many times as you are able. Squats can be done while holding onto the back of a stable chair or with your back against a wall for stability. Strengthening exercises should be done every other day.

In addition to range of motion and strengthening exercises, seniors of all ages should also get some aerobic activity to build muscle and increase stamina. Walking, swimming, and water aerobics are easy on the joints, which make them good choices for those with joint pain. Aerobic exercise should be performed for 30 minutes three times a week, but studies show that bouts of activity done in 10-minute segments can still be beneficial. Of course, if you are currently experiencing joint pain or have not been active, you should consult a physician before beginning any exercise program.

### Food as Medicine

The word medicine is defined as the science and art of healing by *diagnosis*, *treatment*, and *prevention* of disease. When we think of medicine, we tend to focus on diagnosis and treatment, with the aid of physicians and medication, especially as we get older and health issues begin to multiply. Meanwhile, the third and perhaps most important part of that definition—prevention—is often overlooked. While it's true that not every ailment can be avoided, evidence suggests that a majority of health problems can be prevented by lifestyle choices, such as exercise and diet. Now, you may be thinking that it's too late for someone in their 80s or 90s to change their eating habits and make a meaningful difference in their health, but as our bodies face some of the challenges associated with aging, food becomes one of our greatest allies.

In addition to being tasty, comforting, and nourishing, food can serve as preventative medicine. Even if you have health issues such as diabetes, hypertension, or cardiac problems and are taking medication to control these conditions, a healthy diet can help those medications work more effectively and may prevent worsening symptoms. Good food choices can also stave off some of the problems we associate with getting older and make us feel better.

Conversely, without proper nutrition, seniors can become thin and frail, which makes us more prone to injury. Poor nutrition can also lead to digestive problems, such as diarrhea and constipation, and even serious conditions such as bowel obstructions. And finally, an inferior diet can weaken the immune system, which may already be less robust due to age.

Sadly, many seniors fall into poor eating habits, particularly those who are living alone. Cooking for one can be challenging, so we might decide "why bother?" In addition, mobility issues can make preparing meals more difficult. For some, safety concerns hinder their ability to cook. And for others, their appetite may dwindle due to illness or medications.

To overcome some of the obstacles to eating right that many seniors face, Susan Weiner, Registered Dietitian/Nutritionist, suggests the following tips:

- **Companionship** can be an important ingredient. If you

don't like eating alone, try to combine social activities with meal times. Whether you invite a friend to join you for dinner or attend a potluck at the local community center, eating with others can make mealtimes more enjoyable and often improve appetite. You're also more likely to eat a full, balanced meal instead of snacking.

- **If you're having trouble preparing meals for yourself,** don't be afraid to ask for help. There are many food home delivery programs such as Meals on Wheels and those offered by local community centers. In addition, many grocery stores will deliver food to your home. You can also contact your local senior center or adult day center and ask if they offer meal programs. It's a great way to meet other seniors and share a meal along with some conversation.
- **Let family and friends know** that you are having difficulty cooking and ask them to prepare extra servings, which can be frozen and then reheated throughout the week.
- **If necessary, hire someone** to help with food shopping or cooking. If cost is an issue, call your local hospital, church, senior center, or veteran's association to see if there is a trustworthy volunteer in your area who might be able to help.
- **Consider an independent or assisted living community** that not only provides meals, but also allows you to eat in a dining room with others.
- **If you're experiencing a loss of appetite,** check with your physician to make sure there are no underlying health problems. Certain medications can also reduce appetite

and even change the taste of some foods. Switching medications or taking the medication at a different time of the day may solve the problem. There are also appetite stimulants that can be prescribed in severe cases. Our metabolism slows as we age and so does our activity level, so appetite may naturally decrease. Eating smaller meals frequently throughout the day, instead of three large meals, may be more appetizing and easier to digest.

- **For those who are underweight** or having trouble eating balanced meals, add a liquid nutritional supplement to your daily diet.

"In addition to eating balanced meals, the two best things a senior can do to improve their diet are to increase fiber and drink plenty of water," says Weiner. "A lack of fiber can increase your chances of becoming constipated, which tends to happen as we age and is often a side effect to medication. However, when you increase your fiber intake, you must also consume more water. Many seniors aren't naturally thirsty and can easily become dehydrated, so drinking water at regular times throughout the day is important."

A variety of colorful fruits and vegetables, whole grain foods, and beans are good sources of dietary fiber. For those who may have trouble chewing or digesting raw fruits and vegetables, try steaming or roasting vegetables and poaching or baking fruits. Soups and stews, loaded with veggies and beans or whole grain noodles, are also good options.

If you're a caregiver for an elderly person with dietary issues, Weiner suggests looking at the whole person. There is no "one size fits all" diet for seniors. We need to consider an individual's likes and dislikes, overall health, what type of support system they have, their finances, and mental well-being. Eating problems are often due to underlying issues, such as depression or a lack of activity or social interaction. So before we can tackle a dietary problem, we must first address the root cause.

### *A Loss of Taste*

Many seniors complain that food tastes bland and therefore becomes unappetizing. It's true—as we age, our sense of taste does diminish, along with our sense of smell, which is closely connected. First, our tongue has taste buds and receptors that allow us to perceive five flavors: sweet, sour, salty, bitter, and umami (savory). At birth, we have approximately 10,000 taste buds scattered around the tongue, as well as the sides and roof of our mouth, but after age 50, they become less sensitive and begin to disappear. Second, when we eat, food releases odors that engage the olfactory nerves in our nose. These aromas combined with the tastes on our tongue contribute to our overall enjoyment of food. It's also why our sense of smell can warn us of spoiled food. With aging, the nerves in the nose tend to degenerate, decreasing the ability to smell and, therefore, taste. This loss of taste occurs gradually over time and differs by individual. Unfortunately, there is no way to reverse the process.

Losing our sense of taste can negatively affect our health in a number of ways. We may try to compensate for the loss by adding more salt or sugar to our food, which boosts flavor and stimulates taste buds. This could explain why so many seniors begin to crave sweets. Another result is a loss of appetite, which can lead to unhealthy weight loss and lack of nutrition. Though we can't regenerate our sense of taste, there are some things we can do to make eating more enjoyable:

- **Eat with other people** as much as possible. When dining is part of a social event, our appetites tend to increase and we are more likely to eat a variety of foods.
- **Experiment with different flavors,** types of foods, seasonings, and spices. You don't have to use "hot" or spicy flavorings, which may irritate your stomach; spices such as cinnamon, nutmeg, and paprika, along with herbs such as basil, oregano, and thyme, will increase flavor significantly. However, do not rely on salt to boost flavor! Excess sodium may lead to hypertension or make high blood pressure worse in some people.
- **If you're craving sweets,** that's okay. Just be sure not to substitute sweets for healthy foods. Eat balanced meals that include lean proteins, whole grains, and vegetables first. Then, if you enjoy sweets, treat yourself to a small serving of ice cream, a cookie, or slice of pie.

### A Sweet Treat with Benefits

To satisfy a craving for sweets, in a healthy way, try this tasty milkshake recipe. Not only does it provide a daily dose of calcium and vitamin D, it has the added benefit of fiber.

  1 cup low-fat chocolate milk
  2 tsp powdered fiber supplement, such as Benefiber
  1 cup frozen chocolate or vanilla yogurt (or plain yogurt)
  ¼ tsp. cinnamon
  ½ tsp vanilla extract
  3–5 ice cubes

First, stir the powdered fiber supplement into the chocolate milk. Mix well. Put all the ingredients into a blender and blend until smooth, but still thick. Pour into a glass and enjoy!

While a diminishing sense of taste is a normal part of the aging process, any sudden or significant change in taste or appetite should be evaluated by a physician. It could indicate a health problem. In addition, many prescription drugs can change the taste of food or decrease appetite. In some cases, changing your prescription can solve the problem. Dry mouth, which is a side effect of certain medications, can also affect the taste of food. If you're experiencing this condition, try using mouth rinses and lozenges that moisten the mouth.

### Don't Forget the Dentist

Healthy teeth and gums are an important part of aging well. They allow us to eat a wide variety of foods that contribute to a nutritionally balanced diet. Mouth pain, tooth loss, and ill-fitting dentures can make eating painful and difficult, which may lead to weight loss and other problems. Be sure to make regular dental appointments, and keep brushing and flossing daily to maintain good oral health. If you have dental work done, take any antibiotics the dentist prescribes until they are gone, in order to prevent infections. This is particularly important for cardiac patients, as infections can easily spread to the heart.

### Take as Directed

It's fairly common for seniors to take multiple prescription medications for conditions such as hypertension, arthritis, or cardiac problems. In fact, the average senior takes seven different medications, which may include prescription and over-the-counter (OTC) drugs. While these medications can do wonders for maintaining our health, it's important to take them as directed (i.e., do not skip doses, take at the same time each day, take with or without food). Yet, a large number of seniors are not benefitting from their medications and, in some cases, impairing their health by not following the directions on the label. It's estimated that almost two-thirds of seniors make some kind of error when taking their medications. They may forget to take a pill, skip a dose and then take double, or ingest a drug on an empty stomach because they aren't feeling hungry. In some cases, they simply decide to stop taking a particular medication. The reasons for this noncompliance may include: "I don't like the side effects," "I felt better," "It doesn't work," or "It's too costly."

Whatever the case may be, taking medications improperly can have serious consequences. According to government estimates, more than 125,000 people die annually from a failure to properly take medications, while many more are hospitalized. Some of this medication mishap can be prevented by better patient education. Before you or a loved one leaves the physician's office with a new prescription, be sure to ask the following questions:

- **What** is this medication (name and dosage) and what is it for?
- **How** does it work?
- **What are the possible side effects** and how long do they typically last?
- **How many times** do I take it each day and at what intervals?
- **Should** the medication be taken on an empty stomach or with food?
- **Are there any dangerous interactions** with other drugs or certain foods?
- **How long** do I have to take it?"

Many people are reluctant to ask their physician too many

questions, but it's important to clearly understand what you are taking and how to take it properly before you get a prescription filled. Once you are home, there are some tools and tips to help ensure that medications are taken properly:

- **Use an organized pill box,** with separate sections for each day of the week. Some pill boxes are also organized by time of day, such as AM and PM. Fill the pill box up at the beginning of each week and make note of any prescriptions that are getting low.
- **For medications** that must be taken at the same time each day, set an alarm for the scheduled time. There are a number of gadgets available that provide both visual and sounding alarms. Taking a pill with the same meal each day or making it part of your morning or bedtime routine are other ways to stay on track.
- **If you know you are going** to be out of the house, be sure to bring your medication in a travel case so you can take it at the appropriate time.
- **If a drug is supposed to be taken with food,** keep the bottle on the kitchen counter as a visual reminder and take it with a regular meal. If you're out and about, be sure to bring a snack with you to eat along with your scheduled dose.
- **Never discontinue medications** or change dosages without consulting your physician.
- **Be sure to ask your physician** or pharmacist about possible drug interactions or special precautions (e.g., no alcohol, no citrus).
- **If you are having trouble remembering** to take your medications as prescribed, consider the help of a home

aide, or ask a family member to set up a reminder system. Though expensive, there are some new, sophisticated reminding/dispensing systems on the market, as well as phone reminder services. In addition, most independent and assisted living communities offer medication management services, which is one major advantage to consider.

• **Keep an up-to-date list** of all medications and dosages in your purse or wallet, in case of emergency. A family member or caregiver should also have a copy of this list. If you are taken to the hospital, this list will help the doctors with diagnosis and treatment, particularly if you are unable to communicate or have difficulty remembering.

*When Sara's mom began forgetting to take her medications, she bought a pill box at the local pharmacy. The container had a section for each day of the week, as well as morning and evening dividers. Every Sunday evening, Sara filled the pill box with the appropriate medications, which kept her aware of any prescriptions that needed to be refilled, as well as whether her mother was taking her medication as directed. This system helped, but it didn't solve all the problems.*

*"My mom was sometimes confused by which pills were which, and what they were for," explained Sara. "She had six different medications to take throughout the day, and would sometimes forget a dose. If you're having trouble identifying a pill, there's a risk of taking the wrong medication and overdosing. It made me so worried."*

*To help remind her of scheduled dosages, Sara bought a clock radio with dual alarms and put it on her mom's kitchen counter. She set one alarm for 9:00 A.M. for the morning pills and one for 9:00 P.M. for the evening dosages. There was one medication that needed to be taken in the afternoon, as well, so Sara set the alarm on her own mobile phone for 3:00. When her phone* beeped, she gave her mom a quick reminder call. It was also a good way to check in on her during the day.

To ease the confusion regarding her medications, Sara made a chart for her mom. "I got the idea from one of my son's school projects, which identified leaves," said Sara. "I actually glued one of each pill to a piece of poster board, and wrote the name of the drug and what it was for underneath. I also listed the dosage and directions. This was much easier for my mom to see at a glance rather than fumbling with six individual pill bottles. She could look at the chart and see that the oval white pill was for her blood pressure and the round one with the blue lettering was for pain, and so on."

As it turned out, Sara's chart was also helpful to the EMS responders who came to her mom's aid when she had a mild cardiac episode. In the midst of a stressful situation, it was easy to hand the chart over to the paramedic requesting information, rather than trying to remember a long, complicated list of medications and dosages.

### Don't Be Embarrassed

*Ilene had been dealing with her urinary incontinence for a number of years by staying close to restrooms (and using them frequently) and limiting her fluid intake. But over time, the problem became worse, and soon she was saying no to invitations and staying home in order to avoid a humiliating accident. Though she felt trapped by her incontinence, she never thought to discuss it with her physician.*

*"I was embarrassed to talk to him about it," admitted Ilene. "And besides, I didn't think there was anything he could do."*

Ilene is not alone. More than 25 million Americans suffer from urinary incontinence, and many of those folks find it difficult to talk about and therefore suffer in silence. However, it's important to discuss the problem with your healthcare professional and get help. Incontinence can be embarrassing, uncomfortable, and costly. Some estimates suggest that elderly women, who may already be on a limited income, will spend close to $100 a month on protective garments.

"It's a common problem, and I promise you are not going to be the first person to bring it up to your physician," says Dr. Benjamin Brucker, a urologist who specializes in incontinence. "Even if you think you're not that bothered by it, bring it up because it can sometimes be a sign of an underlying medical issue or lead to other health problems. For instance, worsening incontinence may indicate a urinary tract or bladder infection, which requires treatment. Incontinence can also cause painful skin breakdown from constant wetness, while withholding fluids to avoid accidents can lead to dehydration."

Today, there are many products available to help the situation, including medication to calm overactive bladders and protective undergarments, which have improved significantly over the years. In addition, certain foods and caffeinated beverages, such as coffee and tea, can exacerbate the problem and should be avoided. Pelvic floor exercises may also improve the condition (see chapter 4). Begin by discussing the problem with your physician and exploring all the options.

## A Little Peace of Mind

We've all seen the commercials: "I've fallen and I can't get up!" Over the years, these ads for a medical alert product have become the source of many jokes, but the subject is nothing to laugh about. Anyone living alone, not just those with health problems or mobility issues, should invest in a medical alert system, such as Lifeline or 5Star Urgent Response. Accidents and medical emergencies can occur without warning and leave us incapacitated or worse. A simple push of a button can mean the difference between life and death.

Medical alert systems provide peace of mind for both seniors and their loved ones. There are many systems from which to choose, so be sure to do some research before investing. Having numerous choices allows you to select a system that best fits your needs. For example, some systems only work within your home, while others offer remote access, going where you go. Some products contact only emergency medical services, while others also notify an appointed family member. (For tips on making your home safer, see chapter 4.)

## Money Matters

It's not as fun as celebrating a birthday or anniversary, but making a financial checkpoint conference an annual event is a good idea. Experts recommend taking a look at your finances, including monthly expenses, income streams, savings accounts, and investments, on a regular basis—as well as reviewing/revising your budget. Making an appointment with your financial advisor can serve as a reminder, but it can also be done at home. In many cases, this financial review should involve adult children or other caregivers. Although many children are reluctant to talk to parents about finances, it's important to have an honest conversation and be informed about options. Surveys show that many seniors and their caregivers are not well-educated regarding the costs of living options, including home care. For instance, did you know that Medicare does not pay for extended nursing home stays or assisted living?

Too often, we receive a crash course in these subjects after an illness or injury forces us to consider care alternatives. It's much better to research the costs of home aides, assisted living, and other long-term care options before they become necessary and plan for them accordingly. Are you considering or already receiving assistance from home aides? If so, these costs should be factored into financial projections. Is assisted living an option? If so, have you researched the costs? How long can you afford this option? How does the cost of assisted living compare to hiring adequate home care? Are you eligible for Medicaid or other forms of financial assistance? Do you have long-term care insurance? These are just some of the questions to consider when assessing finances and making care decisions.

Because these issues can be complicated, you may want to consider the services of a geriatric care manager or social worker. These professionals can help you determine the amount and kind of care you need, as well as guide you through available programs, services, and eligibility applications. Having a third party is particularly helpful when determining the type of care you may need, as most seniors tend to underestimate how much assistance they require.

## Legal Issues

We've already discussed, in detail, the importance of having advanced medical directives, including a living will and durable power of attorney, but if you haven't gotten around to creating these legal documents, now is the time! If not for yourself, then do it for those you love. Having your estate in order should be considered a gift to your children and other loved ones, alleviating them of the burden of making difficult decisions without your input or dealing with legal battles.

If you haven't done so already, you may also want to consider a DNR or do not resuscitate form. A DNR, also called a No Code or Allow Natural Death, is an official document that allows medical workers to legally withhold resuscitation efforts, such as CPR or advanced cardiovascular life support (ACLS), per your wishes. What many people don't realize is that a living will stating your DNR wishes is usually not sufficient. Emergency and hospital medical staff in most states are still required and/or trained to give CPR or ACLS if a separate DNR doesn't exist.

To make sure your wishes are carried out in all circumstances, you must have a DNR signed by your physician. Unlike advanced directives and durable power of attorney that can come in different forms and even be drawn up by you, a DNR is a state-specific form that all physicians must use in that particular state. In most states, you cannot create a DNR on your own; instead, you must obtain an official form from your physician's office. Additionally, a copy of this form must be on file at each medical facility or on your person.

As we've discussed, it's important to share your end-of-life wishes, as well as the details of these legal documents, with loved ones and caretakers before a health crisis occurs. If you're a caregiver finding it hard to broach this subject, ask a physician or social worker to bring it up. Sometimes the perspective and advice of a third party can open the door to a meaningful discussion.

## Staying Vibrant

The three key ingredients to maintaining vibrancy as we age are socialization, mental acuity, and mental well-being. Though each contributes individually to the aging process, the benefits also intertwine.

### *Socialization*

By now, you should be familiar with this mantra: socialization is important to aging well. Of course, as we get older and our social networks shrink, it can be difficult to heed this advice. It requires a little extra effort to maintain strong social ties with family and friends, but the benefits are certainly worth it, including reduced stress, a more positive outlook, mutual support, and healthier habits—not to mention making life more enjoyable! You can stay socially connected by:

- **Taking advantage** of your local community center or senior center, including transportation services. These facilities typically offer a wide range of activities and events geared toward seniors, from poker games to fitness classes.
- **Joining a club**—there is one for virtually every interest. Look for clubs at church, in senior centers, or online.
- **Considering an adult day program**—Many folks assume these programs are only meant for seniors who need help with daily tasks, but they offer opportunities for social

## Giving Up the Car Keys

Do you remember the excitement you felt when you first started driving? Few things offer the same sense of freedom and independence that getting behind the wheel of a car does. So, it's easy to understand why giving up that independence is such a difficult decision. Not surprisingly, most seniors express a strong desire to continue driving as long as possible. However, for many, there comes a time when driving is no longer safe. How do you know when that time comes?

For the most part, seniors are some of the safest drivers on the road—AAA reports that people in their 50s and 60s have some of the lowest crash rates, and experienced drivers are more likely to engage in safe driving practices such as wearing seat belts, using signals, and adhering to speed limits. On the other hand, driving involves many skills that can be affected by age-related changes, such as vision, hearing, reflexes, arm and leg strength, and cognitive function.

Experts are quick to point out there is no "magic" age at which a driver becomes unsafe. The ability to drive is a result of a person's overall health and fitness, which differs by individuals as they age. The National Highway Traffic Safety Administration notes that it's usually an underlying medical condition, disability, or the side effects of medication that affects a senior's driving abilities, rather than chronological age. Therefore, age should not be used as the sole indicator when determining one's ability to drive safely.

To help you evaluate your driving skills as you age and, in some cases, improve those skills, AAA offers several free tools, including:

- **An Online Self-Rating Form**—It only takes a few minutes to honestly answer this short list of questions, such as: Do you signal and look over your shoulder when changing lanes? Do intersections bother you because there is so much to watch for in all directions? Do you find it difficult to merge with traffic on a busy freeway? Are my children or other family members concerned about my driving? Once you've completed the assessment, you receive suggestions for making improvements.

- **Roadwise Rx**—This online tool provides confidential, individualized feedback about medication side effects and interactions, and how these might affect driving abilities.
- **Free Car Fit Clinic**—Make an appointment at your local AAA office with a trained technician and occupational therapist to help you find the ideal vehicle fit for your comfort and safety.
- **Drivesharp.com**—This computer-based software program with interactive exercises has been clinically proven to help seniors monitor multiple moving objects, see more of their surroundings, and spot and react to possible risks with more confidence.
- **Senior Refresher Courses**—Available at AAA offices and online.

To learn more about these free tools, as well as other helpful tips, visit www.seniordriving.aaa.com.

Since changes in our driving abilities can occur slowly over time, it's advisable to evaluate them often and adjust driving habits accordingly. For instance, as we age, our eyes need more light to see—60-year-old eyes need three times as much light as 20-year-old eyes! This makes it difficult to see objects in the dark. Our eyes also become more sensitive to sunlight and night glare. These changes don't necessarily mean you have to give up driving; it simply suggests that steps should be taken to improve safety. You may decide to limit driving at night, for example, or invest in some high-quality sunglasses. Adjusting your speed to the "reach" of your headlights is also a good idea. Avoiding peak traffic hours and crowded freeways is advisable if you notice a change in your driving skills.

If you're a caregiver who is concerned about the safety of a loved one, the first step is to do a "ride along" to assess the situation. Be on the lookout for these common warning signs:

- Does the driver ever confuse the gas and brake pedal or have difficulty working them?
- Does the driver ignore or miss stop signs or other traffic signals?
- Does the driver weave between or straddle lanes, or fail to check mirrors for blind spots?

- Does the driver get honked at or passed frequently even in slow-moving traffic?
- Does the driver get easily lost or disoriented?
- Has the driver received more than two traffic tickets or warnings in the past two years, or been involved in two or more collisions or "near misses" in the past two years? Rear-end crashes, parking lot fender-benders, and side collisions while turning across traffic are the most common mishaps for drivers with diminishing skills.

If your parent or other senior driver is exhibiting any of these warning signs, it's time to have an honest conversation about giving up the car keys. This can be a very difficult subject to broach, so it should be done compassionately and respectfully. Listen to the driver's concerns and be supportive. The fear of losing one's independence can lead to strong reactions, so be sure to respond with empathy. The focus should be on keeping the driver and others safe.

One way to help ease the transition is to provide some alternative transportation options. You can offer to chauffeur, if possible; research senior transportation services (available at many community centers); and look into volunteer driving programs. It can also be helpful to use one of these transportation services together initially, until the senior is comfortable with the service. This may also be a good time to consider an independent or assisted living community that offers free transportation. Knowing that they can still get out and about may make the decision to give up the car keys a bit easier.

interactions to all seniors. Additionally, some provide meal programs so seniors can dine with friends, and others facilitate organized outings.

- **Planning regular dates** with family or friends, rather than leaving it up to chance. We all know those plans "to get together some time" can fail to materialize unless we put a date on the calendar. Why not plan Sunday dinners with the family and Thursday matinee movies with the ladies?

- **Using technology**—Products such as amplified phones can help those with hearing problems talk to loved ones more easily, and computers designed just for seniors can make it simple to communicate with friends and family. While today's social media sites cannot replace face-to-face meetings, they can help seniors stay in touch with the happenings of family members.

### *Mental Acuity*

As we've learned, engaging and exercising the brain can stave off memory loss and dementia. You can think of these activities as strength training for your brain! To stay mentally sharp, seniors can:

- **Be tech savvy**—Technology is not just for youngsters. Learning or improving your computer skills is a great way to exercise your brain and stay socially connected. If using a computer is difficult, consider one designed specifically for seniors, which features larger keys and simpler formats.
- **Play brain games**—There are a wide variety of games designed to improve mental acuity—and since each region of the brain responds to different types of stimuli, the most effective way to keep the brain fit is to do a variety of activities, from puzzle-solving to memory games. You can download apps for your smartphone, check out websites such as luminosity.com, or simply play video games with your grandkids. For those who

are not tech savvy, try doing crossword puzzles, sudoku, word searches, and playing traditional board games.

- **Learn something new**—It's never too late to learn a different language, play a musical instrument, or try a new craft. The process of learning a skill gives the brain a great workout!

## Mental Well-Being and Depression

The effects of aging and the changes that often come with time—loss of independence, death of loved ones, fewer social connections, failing health—can lead to depression. Though many seniors do suffer from depression, it's estimated that only about 16 percent of those affected receive adequate treatment.

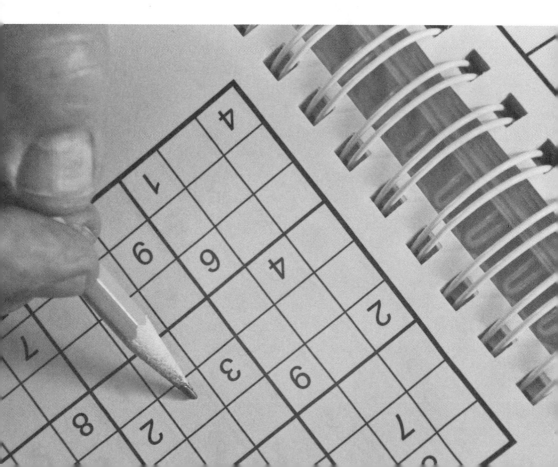

Depression can be difficult to diagnose, and among the elderly it's often overlooked by physicians and caregivers, and may not be recognized by seniors themselves. It's common for seniors to:

- **Assume** they have good reason to be down or depressed, or that depression is just part of aging.
- **Feel isolated,** which in itself can lead to depression, with few around to notice their feelings or discuss them.
- **Not realize** that their physical symptoms are signs of depression.
- **Be reluctant** to talk about feelings or ask for help.

However, depression is not an inevitable part of aging. It's a serious condition that can drain you of energy, disrupt sleep, affect appetite, negatively impact your physical health, hinder relationships, and even lead to suicide. Depression can and should be treated with therapy, medication, and self-help techniques. Treating depression can also help other conditions. For instance, antidepressants are often effective in providing relief to those with chronic pain. Treatment can also improve eating habits and boost activity levels, thus preventing further health issues.

The first step is recognizing potential symptoms and seeking help. Seniors and their caregivers should consult a geriatric specialist if they notice any of the following signs of depression, lasting more than a few weeks:

- insomnia
- loss of appetite
- withdrawal from family and friends
- loss of interest in hobbies and activities
- feelings of helplessness or worthlessness
- mood swings

• fixation on death or suicidal thoughts.

It's also important to understand the causes behind depression. For seniors, it may be related to health problems, such as illness or disability, chronic pain, cognitive decline, or recent surgery. Feelings of loneliness and isolation from living alone or decreased mobility may be the source. For some, having a reduced sense of purpose or anxiety over financial issues can lead to depression. The death of friends, family members, and even beloved pets can often trigger the condition. Recognizing the underlying causes can help treatment be more successful, and in some cases prevent depression from setting in. For instance, if loneliness is an issue, moving to an assisted living facility that provides social opportunities might be a step in the right direction.

Seniors should also keep in mind that many symptoms of depression are a side effect of certain commonly prescribed drugs, including some beta blockers, blood pressure medications, and sleeping pills, to name a few. Your risk increases if you're taking multiple medications. While the mood-related side effects of prescription medication can affect anyone, older adults are more sensitive because, as we age, our bodies become less efficient at metabolizing and processing drugs. If you begin feeling depressed after you start a new medication, consult with your physician immediately.

To keep depression at bay, experts suggest focusing on what you are able to do, instead of dwelling on what is being lost. If you love books, for example, but are finding it difficult to read, start listening to books on tape (available free at most libraries). If one activity or hobby becomes too arduous, ask yourself what you can replace it with? Adapting to changes and finding new things to enjoy can go a long way toward maintaining happiness. In addition, staying physically and socially active and feeling connected to your community, your faith, and your loved ones can ward off depression. Therapists also recommend getting enough sleep, eating a healthy diet, doing volunteer work, taking care of a pet, and praying or meditating as ways to prevent depression or alleviate symptoms.

Remember, depression is not a sign of weakness. It can happen to anyone beginning at a young age and throughout life, regardless of your background. But, you don't have to let it keep you from enjoying your senior years. With the proper treatment and support, you can feel better and live a vibrant life.

## The Power of Pets

If you've ever come home to the joyous, tail-wagging greeting of a dog or stroked the soft fur of a warm cat curled up on your lap, then you already know that spending time with a beloved pet can lift your spirits and reduce stress. But if you need scientific proof, there is plenty of data that show pets provide significant health benefits, both physiologically and emotionally. While these benefits apply to people of every age, they may be especially advantageous to seniors.

Studies have shown that human-animal interactions produce a chemical change in the brain that helps to lower levels of cortisol, a stress-inducing hormone, while increasing the production of serotonin, which makes us feel good. In fact, numerous studies, including one published in the *Journal of the American Geriatrics Society (JAGS)*, indicate that seniors with pets exhibit better physical health and mental well-being than those without animal companions. Specifically, studies show that seniors with pets are more active, visit the doctor less often, have lower blood pressure and cholesterol levels, and are better able to cope with stress. And the effects are immediate: When people handle animals, their blood pressure, heart rate, and body temperature decrease.

Pets can enhance the lives of seniors in many ways. First, animals entail responsibility, which is motivating. Pets need walking, feeding and grooming and encourage playing and petting, all of which require their owners to be active and engaged. Seniors who are physically able are encouraged to take daily walks with their dogs. For those who are less mobile, even simple activities such as getting up to let the dog out or dangling a toy mouse for the cat can prompt more movement.

Emotionally, pets provide companionship, which for many seniors may be in short supply. Everyday interaction with a beloved pet is a powerful way to prevent depression, while caring for an animal provides a sense of purpose, which is a major contributor to aging well. In addition, seniors who care for a pet are more likely to maintain a consistent schedule, which often motivates them to eat and sleep regularly.

Considering these positive aspects, it's no surprise to find many hospitals, nursing homes, rehabilitation facilities and hospices tapping into the power of pets. There are a growing number of pet therapy programs around the country that bring approved animals into these facilities to give seniors a chance to pet and play with them. While the effects may not be scientifically measurable, any staff or family member who has witnessed these interactions can attest to the positive difference it makes to residents. Many senior communities also allow residents to have pets, and some offer special services to help seniors care for their companions, such as walking, grooming and transportation to veterinarian visits. Be sure to do some research before deciding on a community. For those who are living at home and need a little help, look for volunteer organizations that can help match seniors with shelter animals, as well as assist with care and expenses.

Sources: *Journal of the American Geriatrics Society*, May 1999; The American Animal Hospital Association (AAHA); Lynette A. Hart, "The Role of Pets in Enhancing Human Well-being: Effects for Older People," in *The Waltham Book of Human-Animal Interaction*, ed. Ian Robinson (Pergamon, 1995), 19.

## Getting the Help You Need

We've talked a lot about choosing to age well and the steps we can take to make our late life healthier and happier. Yet, no matter how carefully we maintain our health and plan for the future, there often comes a time when aging takes its toll and we need to rely on others for our care. There is a tendency for folks to underestimate the amount of care they need and, as a result, wait too long to ask for help. It's important to get the assistance you need from family members, hired aides, or assisted living facilities *before* accidents make the situation worse or health deteriorates. Take, for example, the fact that by the time many people decide to move to an independent or assisted living community their health or mobility issues require more care than these facilities can provide and are therefore no longer an option.

When the idea of assisted living facilities was conceived (in the early 1990s), it was thought that the residents would be relatively healthy, active seniors who needed a little help and wanted to be part of a community. Instead, we tend to stubbornly stay in our homes as long as possible. By the time many seniors consider assisted living, they require a great deal of assistance. In response, a newer option has emerged—the continuing care retirement community (CCRC) or life-care community. These specialized retirement communities offer a range of services from independent and assisted living, to skilled nursing care at one location, allowing seniors to age in place. Typically, residents move into a CCRC while still they are able to live independently. As a person ages and their medical/care needs change, the level of service increases accordingly, eliminating the need to uproot and move residents. Of course, CCRCs are costly and vary widely in the type of living arrangements and amenities they offer.

Whether a senior decides to stay at home (with the assistance of children and/or paid in-home caregivers), move in with family members, or reside in a CCRC, it's important to get the appropriate level of support—before a health crisis or accident occurs. There's a long list of things to consider when choosing the best living/care options, including:

- The type and level of care needed—there's a big difference between getting help with household chores, meal preparation, and bill paying and requiring assistance with bathing, dressing, and eating.
- The availability and willingness of children or other family members to provide care.
- The personality and preferences of the senior—Is social interaction important? Would he or she participate in and

benefit from organized activities or social opportunities?
- The safety and accessibility of the home or ability to make it safe.
- Financial means.

Finding the best solution requires thorough research into all the available options and, often, some trial and error. However, the most important element in the decision-making process is communication. Seniors and their caregivers should begin with an open conversation, honestly assessing the needs and wants of the senior, as well as those of the caregiver. But don't stop there—caregiving is an ongoing process that requires good communication throughout.

## Finishing Touches

In today's digital age, actual blueprints are a thing of the past. Yet, because they're so engrained in our culture, the term is still widely used to refer to any type of plan (even by youngsters who have never seen a blueprint!). For me, blueprints hold a special place in my heart. My dad, who worked in construction for nearly 40 years, often brought rolls of the drawings home to review, along with his hard hat and work gloves. "Every successful project begins with a good plan," he would say. Of course, he would also be the first to tell you that plans often change! His stack of blueprints typically included many pages of revisions, requiring flexibility and a good attitude.

The same can be said of aging well. Having a framework for managing our finances and legal issues, maintaining our health, and staying vibrant is a good place to start. Plans give us guidance, serve as reminders, and keep us on track when we stray too far from our goals. But when life presents us with challenges, as it tends to do, we must be willing to revise our plans and adapt. The people featured in this book are prime examples of those able to roll with the changes and maintain a positive outlook, while living life with meaning and purpose. We are, after all, works in progress—with opportunities to learn, grow, and contribute to the world around us every day, no matter our age.

## Words of Wisdom . . .

*Well into her 90s, Esther is a classy, well-dressed woman with a great attitude. Like many women of her generation, she got married early (at the age of 19) and considers raising their four children her greatest accomplishment.*

*"I was so young when I got married," recalled Esther. "At the time I didn't even have enough sense to come in out of the rain. Everyone has to work out their own destiny, even if they have to do it the hard way. Eventually they will manage," she added wisely.*

*In retrospect, Esther has a few regrets: "How does anybody look back at their lives and not have regrets? For me, my biggest regret was that I was too judgmental, but with age comes tolerance."*

*Throughout her life, Esther has chosen to read uplifting, affirmative books, believing that positive input translates into positive output. She realized early on that she could choose what information to think about, and by carefully screening the material she allowed into her mind, she was able to focus on the good things in life. This positive outlook has allowed Esther to embrace life to the best of her physical abilities and find joy in simple things. Just being able to walk into the kitchen and make a cup of tea is enough to bring her delight.*

*"I don't anticipate the worst in anything," she said. "I believe I will receive grace to handle anything that happens." With a shrug, she added, "At least I hope so."*

*Esther has some doubts about what the future will hold for her and hopes for a "good death," meaning a very short window of illness, and perhaps being lucky enough to pass in her sleep in her own home.*

*When asked about the secret to living well, she replied, "No matter how ordinary someone's life is, it's the 'nothing things' that make life sweet. For me, it's that first cup of coffee in the morning" With a smile she added: "You know, we can be that first cup of coffee in the morning to each other, and that's the secret of living well."*

# Acknowledgments & Contributors

Every project needs a catalyst. In this case, the task force from CorsoCare set things in motion, armed with a desire to help guide people through the aging process and a long list of factors to consider. In particular, I would like to thank Dan Hughes, Bev Immel, and Wendy Conlon for sharing their vast experience, reviewing text, and providing guidance along the way. Thanks also to Sarah Fenton from Independence Village of Brighton Valley for her insight on the issues facing seniors living in housing communities. Their insight was invaluable.

To my editor, Lynne Johnson, and the staff at Spry Publishing, thanks for your continued support. Lynne is not only a knowledgeable and talented editor, sounding board, and idea-generator, she is also a pleasure to work with, which makes every project more enjoyable.

The heart and soul of this book are really the people and

their stories. Therefore, I must express my sincere appreciation to all those who shared their experiences with me, especially Lydia, Skip, Dorothy, George, and Esther. Their genuine and heartfelt "words of wisdom" serve as both inspiration and education. They are living examples of what it means to age well.

On a more personal note, I would like to thank my husband, Alan, and our son, Sean, for their unconditional love and support. Quite simply, they give my life meaning and purpose—and there's no one on earth I'd rather grow old with! To "the girls," let me just say thanks for demonstrating the importance of socialization. We've never needed studies to confirm that spending time with friends is good for our health.

Finally, this project would not have been possible without the generous time and considerable expertise of the following contributors, who deserve a special note of thanks:

**Christopher J. Berry Esq.** is a certified elder law attorney and VA accredited attorney with the law firm of Witzke, Berry, Carter & Wander PLLC. He has dedicated his practice to helping seniors, veterans, and their families navigate the long-term care legal maze. Attorney Berry has been quoted in *Kiplinger's*, nominated as one of the Best Lawyers in America for Estate Planning & Elder Law by *DBusiness Magazine*, and has received a 10/10, the best rating possible, by AVVO, which ranks attorneys through a peer review process. Attorney Berry is also an Adjunct Professor at Thomas Cooley Law School.

**Dr. Benjamin M. Brucker** is a graduate of the University of Pennsylvania Medical School, where he also completed his internship in General Surgery and residency in Urology. After completing this prestigious residency, he pursued an additional two years of sub-specialization in pelvic organ prolapse, medical and surgical management of incontinence, and voiding dysfunction and neurology in women and men. He is currently practicing at New York University Langone Medical Center in New York City.

**Wendy Conlon, MSPT,** is a licensed physical therapist with close to 20 years of experience. She earned her master's degree from Grand Valley State University in Michigan. Wendy has enjoyed a career filled with clinical experience in both orthopedic and geriatric populations. She spent the last 12 years focused on the functional well-being and rehabilitation of the elderly. Her passion for working with the elderly began in her early childhood when she shared the closest of bonds with her paternal grandparents, who left this world well before their time.

**Michael Johnson** is a Certified Financial Planner®, CPWA®, and partner with Plante Moran Financial Advisors, where he provides comprehensive wealth management services to wealthy individuals and families. Michael has been with the firm since 1991 and has expertise in the following areas: Comprehensive Financial Planning, Investment Management, Estate Planning, and Insurance Planning. Additionally, Michael has extensive experience in manager selection and due diligence as a member of the PMFA Investment Committee. He graduated from Michigan State University.

**Bryan Neal, MS,** is the founder of and Senior Move Manager for Assisted Moving LLC, a professional downsizing and moving service designed specifically for seniors and their families who are relocating to or from a senior community. Prior to starting this company, Bryan had experience working with seniors as an Assisted Living Director and Hospice Territory Marketing Manager, which helped him identify the special needs seniors and their families have when facing a move. Bryan graduated from Central Michigan University with a bachelor's degree in Communications and Psychology, and went on to earn his master's degree in Health Service Administration from the University of Detroit Mercy.

**Susan Weiner, MS, RDN, CDE, CDN,** is a registered dietitian and nutritionist, diabetes educator, and coauthor of *The Complete Diabetes Organizer: Your Guide to a Less Stressful and More Manageable Diabetes Life.* Susan has been named the American Association of Diabetes Educators' Diabetes Educator of the Year for 2015, is the recipient of the 2014 Distinguished Alumna Award from SUNY Oneonta, and was voted one of the top 10 diabetes nutrition education bloggers by iVillage.com. Susan is a member of dLife's medical advisory board and on the advisory board of diabetesisters.org. She earned her master's degree in Applied Physiology and Nutrition from Columbia University.

# Index

hydration, 106, 136

## I

incontinence, 111–14, 144
independence, 20, 128, 149
infectious diseases, 17
inflammation, 80, 82
in-home services
  See also home healthcare
  assessing care needs, 159–60
  insurance coverage for, 74–75
  for meals, 135
  Medicaid benefits for, 71
  supporting aging in place, 129
injury prevention tools and services,
  128–30
insurance
  evaluating needs for, 34, 98
  longevity, 97
  long-term care, 51, 74–75
  medical, 70–73

## J

Johnson, Michael (financial planner),
  34, 50, 95–96
  See also financial advisors
Journal of the American Geriatrics
  Society (JAGS) on pets, 157
Journal of the American Medical
  Association on osteoarthritis, 110–11

## K

Kegel exercises, 113
knee replacement surgery, 109–11
Kroc, Ray, 24

## L

legal issues
  advance health directives, 21–22, 35,
    37–38, 98–99
  attorneys, 38
  living trusts, 99
  living wills, 21, 37, 98–99, 147
  taxes, 52, 99
  wills, 98
  in your 60s, 75–76
  in your 70s, 98–99
  in your 80s and beyond, 147
lessons learned, 8, 10–11
life-care communities, 159
  See also retirement communities
life expectancy, 17, 31, 44
Life Reimagined, 64
lifestyle, 6–7, 8, 48, 133–34
  See also diet; exercise; specific
    medical conditions
living conscientiously, 56
living trusts, 99
  See also legal issues
living wills, 21, 37, 98–99, 147
  See also legal issues
longevity
  American, 18
  Blue Zone findings on, 8, 10–11
  case example of, 20
  desire for, 5–6
  determinants of, 8
  financial resources related to, 19
  insurance coverage for, 97
long-term care insurance, 51, 74–75
loss, 153

**Robin Porter** is a freelance writer and author with firsthand experience as a member of the "sandwich generation." For nearly 10 years, she took on the role of caregiver for her aging parents, while raising a young son. Helping her parents deal with multiple health problems, while navigating the financial, legal, and emotional issues that accompany the aging process, has given her a unique perspective that she shares in this book.

With a background in corporate communications, Robin is an experienced and versatile writer who has produced a wide variety of materials, including annual reports, brochures, newsletters, articles, and press releases. As a freelance writer, Robin has focused her talent on producing nonfiction books. In addition to researching and writing several history/anniversary books for companies such as Domino's Pizza and the Young President's Organization, she has coauthored a number of books on various health-related topics, including *Kids First, Diabetes Second*; *Knock Out Headaches*; *An Ageless Woman's Guide to Heart Health*; and *Living with Juvenile Arthritis*. Though she has developed an expertise in medical topics, she enjoys researching and writing about many subjects.

Robin has a degree in marketing and communications. She lives in Canton, Michigan, with her husband and son, along with their dog.